MS. CHEAP'S
GUIDE TO GETTING
MORE FOR LESS

Mary Hance

RUTLEDGE HILL PRESS®
Nashville, Tennessee
A Thomas Nelson Company

Published by Rutledge Hill Press, a Thomas Nelson Company, P.O. Box 141000, Nashville, Tennessee 37214.

Much of the material in this book first appeared in the "Ms. Cheap" column in *The Tennessean*. It is copyrighted by and used with the permission of *The Tennessean*. Some material was first printed in the *Nashville Banner* and *American Profile* magazine.

Illustrations by Drew White.

Library of Congress Cataloging-in-Publication Data

Hance, Mary, 1953–
    Ms. Cheap's guide to getting more for less / Mary Hance.
      p. cm.
    ISBN 1-55853-724-4
    1. Consumer education. 2. Shopping. I. Title.

TX335 .H3435 2001
640'.73—dc21

00–068854

Printed in the United States of America
2 3 4 5 6 7 8 9—05 04 03 02 01

Ms. Cheap's Guide to Getting More for Less

To my readers, who have generously shared their clever money-saving tips and kindly read mine, and to my wonderful family, who has supported me and put up with all my cheapness

Contents

Introduction ix

Chapter 1   Quiz: How Cheap Are You? 1

Chapter 2   Shopping on the Cheap 4

Chapter 3   Saving on Gift Giving .25

Chapter 4   Saving at the Grocery .35

Chapter 5   Saving at Home 57

Chapter 6   Saving on Family and Fun 103

Chapter 7   Travel for Less 127

Chapter 8   Saving Wherever You Can 136

Chapter 9   Websites and Miscellaneous Tips 155

Chapter 10   Being Cheap to Be Generous 183

Chapter 11   Tips That Are Waaaaay Out There 196

Chapter 12   Ethics Quiz: How Cheap Is Too Cheap? 208

Introduction

Hello, fellow cheapos. My hope is that this book will help you get more for less, that it will help you develop and nurture the mind-set that is thrifty, cheap, frugal, tight, or whatever you want to call it. I also hope that some of it will make you laugh at the degree of cheapness to which some people stoop.

My "Ms. Cheap" column, which appears in *The Tennessean* in Nashville, and this book have the same goal—to offer practical and fun ways to get the most for our money. My writing is not so much for the down and out but for people like you and me who are making decisions every day about what we do with our limited resources. A lot of it is a balancing act between where we want to sacrifice and where we want to splurge. Choices have to be made.

My friend Bonnie Walsh said it best: "I don't mind spending money. I just hate to waste money." That is what this is all about: not wasting our hard-earned money. I have tried to include as many money-saving, penny-pinching tips as possible. Many of them were entries in my newspaper's annual Cheapest of the Cheap contest or ideas submitted by readers for our "Shortcuts" section.

Others came from a contest in conjunction with Goodwill Industries of the Southeast, in which Goodwill shoppers were invited to submit their money-saving tips. If their tips were included in the book, they received a gift certificate to Goodwill. This was underwritten by my generous friend Ruth Ann Leach Harnisch and her Harnisch Foundation. The Goodwill tips are identified by the Goodwill logo.

Obviously not all of these tips will apply to everybody, but I hope most of them will be useful to you. And I want you to know that I have included some really bizarre tips just because I thought you needed to know just how cheap some people are.

I have one disclaimer . . . I do not personally do all of these things. I do most of them, but there are a few that I just write about.

I hope the book enriches and enhances your daily life. And if you know of other money-saving tips, feel free to send them to me at *The Tennessean,* 1100 Broadway, Nashville, TN 37203.

Enjoy my book and, of course, stay cheap!

Acknowledgments

Whenever anyone does anything as ambitious as writing a book, there are a lot of people to thank. Special thanks to *The Tennessean* for allowing me to pursue this opportunity and to Rutledge Hill Press for publishing this book. Many, many thanks to all of you whose tips appear here, and of course, I want to say thanks to all of you, my loyal readers, for buying the book.

I also want to thank my husband, Bill, for his optimistic support of my book project and our daughters, Elizabeth and Anna, for their computer help. Last but not least, I want to thank my parents, Virginia and Brinkley Morton, for showing me in the first place that being thrifty is smart.

1

Quiz: How Cheap Are You?

Are you a cheapskate or merely frugal? Here's the definitive test to determine if you are cheap. Simply answer yes or no to the following questions.

1. Do you shop consignment?
2. Do you shop thrift stores?
3. Do you shop at garage sales?
4. Have you ever had a garage sale?
5. Do you reuse your plastic baggies?
6. Do you water down your liquid soap?
7. Do you use your dryer sheets more than once?
8. Are you a roadside scavenger . . . looking for usable items that may have ended up on the curb?
9. Do you double coupon and/or triple coupon?
10. Do you use store brands?
11. Do you check out all your reading material from the library instead of buying books?

12. Do you check out videos from the library instead of renting them?
13. Do you drink water when you go out to eat?
14. Do you take advantage of the free activities like movies and concerts that your town or city offers?
15. Do you take your own snack to the movies?
16. Do you cook at home instead of going out?
17. Do you take your own lunch to work or school?
18. Do you pay off your credit card in full each month?
19. Do you have a budget?
20. Do you stick to your budget?
21. Do you reuse aluminum foil?
22. Do you take home even the smallest amount of leftovers from a restaurant?
23. Do you save money every month no matter what?
24. Do you check pay phones and or newspaper racks for change?
25. Do you keep all worn out vehicles for spare parts?
26. Do you refuse to throw anything away because you may need it again in seven years?
27. Are you still watching black and white TV?
28. Do you save receipts in hopes that an item will go on sale and you can go back and get the savings?
29. Do you cut paper towels or napkins in half?
30. Do you ask salespeople to call you when something goes on sale?
31. Do you check three places' prices before you buy a major item?
32. Do you take things back if you find them cheaper somewhere else?
33. Do you inspect every bill to be sure there are no errors?

34. Do you watch for scanner errors when you are checking out at stores that offer free or discounted items if the scanner is in error?
35. Do you pick up pennies?
36. Do you resend greeting cards that you get?
37. Do you get excited when you save money????

Now for the assessment:

If you answered yes to twenty-five questions, you are "Certified Cheap"!

If you answered yes to thirty questions, you are "Certified Ultra Cheap"!

If you answered yes to all thirty-seven questions, you are so cheap that you should be writing my column and this book!

2

Shopping on the Cheap

"A Dollar Saved Is a Dollar Earned": How to Curb Your Spending

I once spoke to a Family and Community Education club in Hermitage, Tennessee, and one of the ladies shared with me a handout from the University of Tennessee Agricultural Extension Service called "A Dollar Saved Is a Dollar Earned." My favorite part was a list of questions to ask yourself before you buy an item. I have clipped this out and put it in my wallet to refer to whenever the shopping bug bites, or even nibbles. I also made copies for our two teenage daughters, who were not as thrilled as I was to get this list. Here goes. Before buying an item, ask yourself:

- Can I do without it?
- Can I postpone its purchase?
- Can I substitute something else that costs less?

- Can I shop around for a better deal?
- Can I use my skills to make it?
- Do I already own one?

The list really works remarkably well. The only additional question I would add is, "Can I borrow one?" My personal favorite is the one about postponing a purchase. Almost always, if I tell myself that I will go back to buy something, I get distracted and either don't get there or talk myself out of it. If you decide that you need something or have to have it, the final question to ask yourself is, "Can I shop around and get a better deal?" And the answer is that yes, most of the time you can.

Consignment Shopping

There it is, your closet, stuffed with great clothes you'll never wear again. And since you know you paid a lot for them, you just can't bring yourself to give them away or try a yard sale. What to do? Well, clothing consignment makes a lot of sense.

Consignment shopping is one of my favorite ways to save money. Not only can you buy a "new" wardrobe for yourself at a fraction of the retail cost, but you can also get rid of clothes that you are no longer wearing and recoup some of your investment.

For starters, selling clothes at consignment is a lucrative way to clean out that closet and make room for the new season's fashions. Although you recoup only about one-sixth to one-fourth of what you paid, it's surely better than nothing.

And consignment shopping is one of the most economical ways to buy clothes, too. Generally you pay about a third of what they cost when new. The other big plus of consignment shopping is the service and personal touch on which most of the shops pride themselves. Virtually all of the consignment shops in our area are owned by people who are there day in and day out. They get to know you and your wants and needs.

I talked to veteran consignment shopper/seller Marcie Allen, a booking agent who has consignment down to a science—or maybe an art. Allen started her consignment shopping binges at age fifteen, when she dropped into a chic consignment shop before going on a cruise and bought just about all the shorts they had for sale. Now, ten years later, she goes both ways in the world of consignment—selling her clothes and buying other people's at bargain prices.

> Economy is the art of making the most out of life.
> —George Bernard Shaw

In one of her shining moments, she paid $70 for a consigned long red cocktail dress that originally cost $200. She wore it just once, to a Valentine's Day party, then took it back to the consignment shop and let them resell it for about $50.

"It's recycling," she said with a laugh.

Allen gets excited over particularly big bargains, such as a consigned Anne Klein coat she bought for $95 and then saw an almost identical version in a department store for $325.

"I bring in everything I am sick of and then I can get some more new things," she said.

Some months she gets as little as $13 in consignment sale money.

Marcie Allen started her consignment shopping binges
at age fifteen, when she dropped into a chic
consignment shop before going on a cruise and bought
just about all the shorts they had for sale.

Other months, her check is as high as $275. Either way it is almost certainly more than she could get at a garage sale. The other advantage is that with consignment shops, she has the whole season instead of one weekend to try to sell the items.

Knowing how the consignment system works will give you an edge. If you're selling on consignment:

- Before you load up your clothes, visit consignment stores in which you're interested. Meet the owners and find out how they handle consignors and what's a good time to bring in your clothes. Ask lots of questions, such as how long they've been in business, whether you have to have an appointment to bring things in, how long they keep merchandise before they mark it down, and how many consignors they have.
- Know how much money you'll get for your items and how you'll receive it. Shop owners (not the consignors) typically do the pricing. Many shops offer a 50/50 split, where consignor and the shop each get half of the sale price. Some shops give the consignor only 40 percent, so find out in advance. To get your money, at some stores you must stop by the shop and ask for a check. Others want you to leave self-addressed, stamped envelopes so they can mail checks to you. And some shops will automatically send your money monthly or even twice a month.
- Get your clothes to the shop at the earliest opportunity. If you can get them on the racks as soon as the season starts, shops have more time to sell them.

- Ask what stores do with items that don't sell. Most give you a choice: you pick them up or the store donates them to a charity. You probably would like to know what charity, if that is the route you take. And you may want to give them to charity yourself to get the tax deduction, instead of letting them have it.
- Make sure the items you take are clean and current. Most of the shops are fairly picky; they don't want outdated clothes and certainly don't want things that are dirty or stained. Obviously, the better the clothes look, they better they sell. Plus, it's embarrassing when they reject a bunch of stuff because of spots.
- Deal with more than one consignment shop. Some are pickier than others, so if one store won't take all of your clothes, take the rejects home, clean them up, and try another place.

If you're shopping at consignment stores:

- Shop often. These shops get "new" things in all the time and if you hit it right, you can really get some bargains.
- Get to know the owner/manager/clerks. Ask them to call you if they get a lot of things in your size or if there is something in particular for which you are looking.
- Know brands and retail prices. You must know the retail prices in order to be sure you're getting a good deal.
- Ask if they have coupons; several do from time to time, and they'll save you even more.
- Shop late in the season, when the shops offer further reductions on

the already-good deals. This is where the real steals are. Toward the end of each season, almost every store marks down 25 percent to 40 percent or more, making the price a fraction of the original cost.

Thrift Store Shopping

Thrift stores like Goodwill and Salvation Army are another way to save big time, not just on clothes but on all sorts of other things. Here is what some Goodwill shoppers had to say about what they find in Goodwill stores and why they shop there.

Tips: Thrift Stores

"Buy like-new items at Goodwill or other thrift shops and give them out as Christmas gifts; people will think you paid full price for them." —*Bill Smallman*

"Make a fun day out of shopping at Goodwill. Call two or three friends and make a list of the Goodwill stores in your area. Meet for lunch or breakfast, and take off together for the day. After you have made all the Goodwill stops, have coffee together and show each other all your great buys. It's lots of fun and you will learn something with each trip." —*Dori Klein*

"When I can buy a new book or toy for 25¢, 50¢, or 75¢, why go to a retail store and pay $35 or $50? I do my Christmas shopping all year for family and friends at Goodwill." —*Louise Spencer*

"I love coming to Goodwill because I save so much money and I love what I buy. That way I can save money myself so I can help others." —*Betty Mays*

"One of the best bargains is sheets. Colorful sheets are wonderful sources of fabric for crafts. Aprons, rag rugs, quilt squares, and more can be made from sheets. One sheet may have four or five yards of fabric and is a terrific bargain at Goodwill." —*Denise McCutcheon*

"Buy things at Goodwill for the buttons. The buttons can be used to dress up another outfit. Buttons are very expensive at fabric stores, so this is a way to save money and look good too." —*Gail Stewart*

"I have seen people buying materials for props and clothing for theatrical productions—furniture, drapes, clothing, and just material look great on stage, and you can usually use the item without doing much to it." —*Warren Bishop*

"I look for prom dresses with full skirts. I cut the skirt off, cut a round piece of coordinating fabric, and drape it over a round table. It makes a lovely table cover, and I get all kinds of compliments." —*Eleanor Johnson*

"I purchase certain skirts and dresses for the material. I have made some beautiful pillows with the material—tapestry, silk weaves, etc. Most pillows of these materials sell for $50 to $60 each." —*Donna Bellis*

"The clothes are so cheap that we buy old blue jeans and blue jean skirts to make our own shorts, pants, and shirts." —*Melinda Hamilton*

"I look for books and cassette tapes that can be used for my enjoyment. After reading the books, I resell them at second-hand bookstores. Also I buy clothes and Bibles to donate to the Nashville Union Rescue Mission as tax-deductible gifts." —*Michael Mann*

"Use clothing from Goodwill to decorate garden sculptures and scarecrows." —*C. Burr*

"Buy a kid's sheet at Goodwill and save on wrapping paper by wrapping the birthday present in the sheet and have a sheet left to use on the kid's bed." —*Linda Tinsley*

"Very often I read a book that I love too much to 'loan' to a friend, but by shopping at Goodwill, I can often purchase a second or even a third copy of that same book to share with friends. I tell them to keep it or pass it on." —*June Zaner*

"I have a Victorian bedroom and hang the bouquets over the top of my dresser, along with baby items such as booties, sweaters, and hats. I love shopping at Goodwill. My daughter never needs to buy clothes for my two grandchildren. I'm expecting a third, so I'm shopping for it." — *Eleanor Johnson*

"I have been on nine cruises in the Caribbean, Bermuda, Alaska, and

Mexican Riviera, and I represent Goodwill with about 95 percent of my clothes." —*Mrs. Gene Goodman*

"I buy all the tin cans. I bake cookies, brownies, and cakes for the holidays, and believe it or not, it's cheaper than buying tin foil or baggies." —*Connie Hamilton*

"I search for framed prints and pictures in the housewares area of Goodwill. Older pictures in questionable condition can yield a great frame. I take the good frames and mats to save for nice pictures." —*Jini Nash*

"I never buy clothes at retail price now. I shop the Goodwill outlet and yard sales. It never ceases to amaze me. The good Lord always directs me to the places and the cheapest prices when I need them."—*Martha Plunkett*

"My money is tight. Therefore, I shop at Goodwill, where I find bargains on each visit. Sometimes it may take two or three visits to get exactly what you want. At times you will find a 50 percent off sale that is really treating the consumer right." —*Bill Evans*

"I shop at discount stores (like Goodwill) and get everything I need for the house." —*LaDonna Gadde*

"I buy my computer parts at Goodwill. It is cheap and good. Can't beat it." —*Walter Whitworth*

Margaret Fisher buys baskets for arrangements or for Easter at Goodwill. She also finds sheets that she can turn into curtains.

Michael Carver bought an antique chair for $2 at Goodwill and stripped it and fixed it up for $5.

"I look for old linens to decorate with. I also look for bridal bouquets. I shop at Goodwill and still have money to spend tomorrow to do it all over again. You can find brand-new clothes and retro clothes. I've decorated my entire home with pictures and whatnots for little or nothing." —*Eleanor Johnson*

Jini Nash shops daily at the local Goodwill superstore and stocks up on new items, particularly toys. "I keep these in a spare bedroom, and as gifts are needed, most always I can find a gift to fit. Unused baby clothes are often donated because they are too small, so I grab them for my next shower invitation."

"Shop till you drop!" at Goodwill. — *Nikki Boyd*

Strategies for Garage Sale Shopping

I have to warn you that going to garage sales can be addictive. When my daughters were little, we used to go every week. I was off on Fridays and it was our weekly adventure. You would not believe the things we bought: A gorgeous hooked rug. A Crockpot. Dozens of toys and dolls and games. Plants. Mops and brooms. Dish towels, custard cups, pots and pans. A bicycle. An operating room light. A beanbag chair. A needle-point chair. Tupperware. A flamingo light. Clothes for the whole family. And on and on.

You may think I'm a yard sale junkie, but believe me, I'm in good company, and I have learned a lot from other addicts. So here are my best tips for shopping garage sales:

- Plan your day using the newspaper and a map. Professional "junkster" Maude Gold Kiser says a book map is best so you don't have to unfold it. She also suggests taking a pair of binoculars in your car so you can see the small print on the yard sale signs.
- Never pay the first price marked on an item. Always offer less. James Williams and his mother go to garage sales almost every week, and he says, "Definitely negotiate. They don't want to take it back in the house." Williams's best buy ever was a $600 train set that he bought for $75. "It was practically brand new with the price tags still on some pieces," he bragged. (This is the kind of buy that gets you hooked.)
- Be nice and friendly (as opposed to pushy and rude) when negotiating.
- After negotiating each item, lump your buys together and round the total down. For example, if you have negotiated the price of a T-shirt from $1.00 to $.75, the price of a Crockpot from $6.00 to $4.00, and the price of a light from $1.50 to $1.00, then ask if you can give them $5.00 for the whole lot. They'll probably say yes.
- Don't insult the owner with an embarrassingly low offer like "Will you take a quarter for that antique dresser?"
- If there is something you are looking for, say, a rug or a lamp or a

shovel, ask! Sometimes people forget to put things out or might think of something they didn't know they wanted to sell.

- Ask if there is anything else for sale that isn't already out. Sometimes people are so inundated with early customers they don't get all of their merchandise out at first.
- Be sure you know clothes sizes and measurements of windows and floors, tables, and so on, in case you find something that might fit.
- Go early. The selection is better.
- Go late. The prices are better. Maude Kiser says the later in the day, the better, especially if you are looking for clothes.
- Leave your name and number with an offer. My cheapo brother used to do this, leaving a lowball offer in case, as the day drags on, they are willing to take whatever they can get.
- Have fun. See it as a treasure hunt—because, you know, it really is!

Oh, and the last thing, be prepared to have your own garage sale to get rid of some of the things you bought at other people's sales. Guess what was in the last sale we had: a gorgeous hooked rug, a Crockpot, dozens of toys and dolls and games, plants, mops and brooms, dish towels, custard cups, pots, and pans . . .

Holding Your Own Garage Sale

I have participated in a lot of garage sales over the years, starting with one I had a few years out of college, where our very first customer insulted us by saying our sale looked "picked over." It was 6:30 A.M.

My friend Barbara and I had lots of good stuff—four or five green florist vases, a set of rooster salt and pepper shakers, a makeshift rack full of slightly used clothes, a set of great speakers that could easily be fixed, some really neat mugs, a box full of perfectly good coat hangers, a lampshade, even some books (college textbooks) and records. Perfectly respectable stuff! I wouldn't have sold that annoying man anything at that point.

But as the morning wore on and the customers came and went (without buying anything), we realized the annoying man might have had a point. We closed up shop at noon, just barely making enough money to pay for the ad in the paper and the box of doughnuts to which we treated ourselves as a reward for all our hard work.

Dozens of yard sales later, I know that the first step is to be sure you have enough good stuff to make it worth your time. Look in every room, every drawer, every closet for stuff to sell.

> In my opinion, cheapskate now describes a very classy and dignified individual who saves consistently and spends less than he or she earns.
>
> —Mary Hunt, editor of the *Cheapskate Monthly*

I also learned to seek advice from people who have lots of experience with this quirky breed of retail. Berenice Denton, who has held countless garage and estate sales in Tennessee, says: "Set the sale up so that it has an attractive look. The biggest mistake is to lump things all together and try to get people to buy them as a lot. People like to pick through it. Also, have things checked before slapping a price on them. Find out what things are worth so that you don't get taken."

Another suggestion is to price with hang tags instead of stickers since they don't fall off as easily and people can't change them as easily. (Yes, people do that.)

"The key is preparation, getting things so they look clean and organized," says my friend and former neighbor, Jeanie McKee. "Make a party of it. Join with a friend or neighbor. It makes less work, and more people come for neighborhood sales. Advertise in the newspaper. Serious garage sale shoppers plan their day by looking at the sales in the paper."

Her daughter Katherine McKee says don't get sentimental: "Go with your first impulse" about what to get rid of.

My brother Charles (who loves a good garage sale, much to his wife's dismay) always has a "free pile" where he puts stuff he doesn't want to haul off. You'd be surprised what people will take.

Here are more do's and don'ts:

- DO be ready early no matter what time you start your sale. Serious shoppers are out early.
- DO have plenty of change—coins and dollar bills.
- DO have a portable phone at the sale so you don't have to let people inside your house.
- DON'T put your money down anywhere. Use a tummy pack, apron, or pockets to keep it safe.
- DO negotiate.
- DON'T price whole tables at one price. Price individually, if you can.
- DO price your items to sell.

- DO plan ahead about leftovers. Have someone pick them up or know where to take them.
- DO take names and numbers of people who are interested in big-ticket items and ask them to write down what they would pay. Then you can call them if the item doesn't sell to someone else.
- DO have fun!

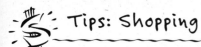

Tips: Shopping

"I never throw away receipts. So many of the stores offer a seven-to-twelve-day adjustment policy. If it goes on sale within those days, take your receipt back to the store and they will give you the difference in the amount back in cash. I have done this many times and have gotten back as much as $32 in one trip." —*Diane Eason*

"Tired of your old wardrobe? Hold an exchange party with friends. Have each person bring several outfits to trade and everyone gets to go home with 'new' clothes." —*Pam Barber*

"More than once I have found a plus-size skirt at a thrift store or garage sale (average cost, 50¢), cut it apart, and made my children clothes from the material. I use the buttons for other outfits too." —*Julie Parker*

"When you shop at a store that has free gift wrapping, have all your purchases gift wrapped, including what you buy for yourself. Then you get a free box, paper, and bow that you can use later." —*Rebecca Graham*

"Buy suits or clothes at Goodwill, and what doesn't work, resell to a consignment shop and get double what you paid." —*Natalie Stone*

"Shop for bridesmaids dresses at yard sales. I bought a $242 dress by Waters and Waters for $15 and then asked the owner where I could contact the other girls to buy their old dresses. This was a real bargain." —*Nancy Ledford*

"Every piece of electronics or furniture I have bought, I have saved money by matching prices with competitors. My wife and I saved over $100 on a mattress and our twenty-seven-inch TV by going back and forth to see if the competitors would match or beat the prices. I went back and forth between two electronics stores for two hours until I got the price I wanted on the TV. If I hadn't gotten the price, I would have left. You've got to be ready to walk away if the price isn't right. Then they will come down a little." —*Clay Dyer*

"Always wait for a garage sale or consignment sale—any and everything at a mall or department store will appear there and at a fraction of the price." —*Victoria Hunt*

"Offer cash instead of a credit card for less cost. It works with small store owners." —*Cathy Sutton*

In the process of getting her house ready to sell, Alice Huang found that shopping around really paid off. "Exterior painting—I got a $2,800 proposal from one company, $4,882 from the other company for a pressure wash and two coats. Another one suggested only sand and one coat for $1,600. I felt it was still too much. So I got pressure wash only for $239 and it looks nice without new painting." Huang reported that the estimates for washing and sealing a driveway ranged from $427 to $1,135.

Dana Bates said she saves hundreds of dollars a year by clever combinations of rebates and coupons. She sent in receipts to show that she had received $116.34 worth of merchandise for $1.32 in cash that she spent.

"I've had times when I wanted to get rid of a number of items, but there were too few to have a yard sale and, anyway, my condo didn't permit them. With my boss's permission, I had an office sale. I put my wares out right after work so that it wouldn't interfere with the work day. No worry about the weather or parking, and no advertising costs. My coworkers cleaned it out within an hour. I have also done this with clothes and jewelry. The best part is that I got to keep all the money instead of splitting it with a consignment store." —*Eleanor Barrett*

"To save money on a yard sale, invite four friends to have one too. Divide the cost of the ad between you." —*Shelia Newman*

"When I see a good coupon on Sunday for free candy, products, etc.,

I go to the recycling bin later and pick out coupon sheets and get lots of extra coupons for the product." —*Tammy Steele*

Beverly Perry and her sixteen-year-old daughter, Rachel, make an award-winning cheap team. Beverly says: "When I began working full-time instead of part-time, I found that I had great difficulty keeping up with my couponing and rebating system. At the same time, my daughter (eleven at the time) wanted to earn extra spending money. I began to pay her a 33¢ commission on all coupons she redeemed and a 50 percent commission on all rebates earned. Our family saved money, our daughter learned valuable money-saving skills she will use as a future adult shopper, and I was able to save valuable family time."

"Research. Don't buy the first thing you see. Read *Consumer Reports*. Decide what you want before you are taken in by the showroom glamour." —*Mary Carter*

"I price-comparison shop. Many stores are happy to match prices—and it saves me the trouble of having to go to another store." —*Liz Romagosa*

"Save all your findings, like pennies on the ground, and purchase an item. It is a good way to save." —*Adriane Nash*

"Buy things at the end of a season for the next year. The store is trying to sell them to get new stuff coming in for the present season." —*Diane Spence*

"Did you know that the Lowe's chain will meet any competitor's price on any item they stock? And will then offer you an extra 10 percent discount on that item?" —*Bill Oehlecker*

"I buy my sandwich bread, hot dog buns, hamburger buns, and other bakery items at bakery outlets. You can get bread for half what you would pay in stores. I buy three or four loaves of bread and freeze it until I need it." —*Elsie Wheeler*

"I pay special attention to the special interests of friends and coworkers. When I find an item that is in the interest range of these people, I buy it and mark it up with a 'finders fee.' They don't mind because they are still getting a good deal and it was brought right to them." —*Jini A. Nash*

"If you buy something that you really don't need, whatever the cost, match it by saving the same amount as you spent on the purchase. You will find that after awhile you won't be spending any unnecessary money." —*Deborah Rector*

"Think about what you need and then shop."
—*Grace Smith*

"Use coupons regularly. Always 'buy-one, get-one-free' when available. Shop dollar stores and yard sales when available."
—*Brenda Leslie*

"When shopping at yard sales, it pays to go later in the day or a couple of hours before they close down. At that time they are more willing to bargain on the prices. Usually things go half price because they do not want to put it all away." —*Kellie Poulsen*

"Don't leave the car with your money. It's more tempting to buy something. Before your purchase, ask yourself, is it really worth going all the way back to the car?" —*Lauren Grisham*

The best money-saving shopping tip is "leave your wife at home." —*Galen Washington*

3

Saving on Gift Giving

How to Cut Back on Gift Giving

Christmas is a time when almost everyone feels pressured to spend. You have a list of people and you feel like you have to buy something for everybody. Maybe, maybe not. There are ways to cut spending without cutting off a relationship. Ways to cut without feeling like el cheapo supreme.

For example, I got a call not long ago from my college roommate, whose daughter is my godchild, and who is godmother to one of our daughters. After all these years of trying to come up with fun gifts for each other's children at Christmas and on birthdays, my friend suggested we just concentrate on birthdays. What a relief. I wish I'd thought of it myself.

Think about other people on your list who might fall into this category—people you don't see as often as you used to and who probably feel just as unnecessarily obligated as you do.

Another savings route is to buy a family gift rather than separate gifts for everyone. A multipurpose game board, volleyball set, or other family game could be just the answer.

The National Center for Financial Education has some tips for smart holidays giving:

- Look for bargains all year—garage sales, antique stores, consignment shops, flea markets.
- Spend cash so you know exactly what you are spending. Keep track of your spending.
- Give gifts that don't require out-of-pocket money—baby-sitting, car washes, yard cleanup, etc. Be creative.
- If you give money, a U.S. Savings Bond costs half its face value.
- If you're looking for a part-time job for the holidays, consider a retailer who gives an employee discount.
- Make gifts at home: baked goods, jellies, arts and crafts.
- Save on greeting cards and postage by sending only to out-of-town friends and relatives.

Speaking of Christmas cards, I'm told there is a man in Dickson, Tennessee, who is even cheaper than I am. I don't know his name (lucky for him), but they say he's is *so cheap* that he addresses his Christmas cards to himself and then puts as the return address the names and addresses of the people to whom he really wants the cards to go. Then he dumps them all in the mailbox—without stamps—and they are all returned to the return addresses. Free mail.

Mind you, I'm not recommending it, but I did want you to know how cheap some people are.

There's Nothing Wrong with Regifting, If You Follow the Rules

A couple of Christmases ago, I got caught regifting. I hate to admit it, but it's true. Here's how it happened. Our great friends Christy and David had given us a lovely basket of pasta, candy, cookies, homemade bread—all kinds of goodies. I got home and unloaded the contents into the pantry and put the basket up. A few days later, I was making up a gift basket for other friends, and the goodies I had wouldn't fit. I grabbed Christy's basket, filled it, and thought nothing more of it.

As luck (bad luck) would have it, Christy was at our house when our other friends came by to share gifts. She couldn't help but notice her basket dancing out the door. Ugh! What could I say, what could I do, but apologize and hope that Christy's sense of humor would prevail, which it did. However, I will never live it down.

I was embarrassed not because regifting is wrong, but rather because I didn't want my friends to feel that I didn't like what they had given me. I didn't want to slight them in any way. But at the same time, I felt that recycling the basket was better than buying another one, when this one was just perfect. There is nothing inherently wrong with regifting if you do it right and if, of course, you don't get caught like I did. The bottom line is what people don't know won't hurt them. Even Miss Manners says it's OK.

Doing it right means giving someone something you have that you truly think that person would like. You don't give your best friend the ugly sweater or tacky earrings somebody gave you three years ago. But you could give a pal the brand-new, still-in-the-box coffee grinder that your aunt gave you last year and you don't want because you already have one. Knowing where it came from shouldn't be important.

In some lights, regifting can be the most thoughtful way to give. For example, a friend's mother gave us a silver bread tray with an "H" engraved on it that had been in her family for two generations. She said nobody in her family ever knew what the "H" was for and that it must have been for "Hance." It wasn't that she was too cheap to buy us a "real" wedding gift, but more that she had something she honestly thought we'd like better than what she could buy. And we do love it.

So I say look around your closets, attic, and basement and see what you have that someone on your list would love. Wrap it up and give it without a tinge of guilt. Regifting just gets a bad rap from people who take it too far, like Cincinnati Reds owner Marge Schott, who a couple of years ago supposedly sent a bouquet of "used" flowers to the umpires' association after the death of one of the umpires.

Ever since man began to till the soil, and learned not to eat the seed grain, but to plant it, and wait for the harvest, the postponement of gratification has been the basis of a higher standard of living and civilization.

—S. I. Hayakawa

Knowing when to regift and when not to is crucial! So here are a few rules:

- Never regift items if you aren't sure what they are, such as labelless homemade canned foods someone gave you the year before that do not have a label.
- Never regift items if you're not sure how old they are, such as a box of candy that you found in a closet from a Christmas past.
- Never regift items if you're not sure who gave them to you. The danger here, obviously, is that you might regift something to the same person who gave it to you to begin with!
- Always check to be sure there are no telltale signs (like a card or note) that will give you away.
- Never regift an item just to get rid of it; regift it only if you think the new recipient will really like it.

Tips: Gift Giving

"My sister and I sometimes share the cost of a wedding shower gift. We purchase a laundry basket or kitchen trash can and fill it with cleaning products that we have purchased with double coupons. It allows us to give more." —*Pam Barber*

If you want to reproduce old family photographs and portraits but want to avoid the expense and possible copyright problems, here is a way. "I decided to take a picture of the picture with my own thirty-five-millimeter camera. Now I can quickly and cheaply reproduce any five-by-seven or larger portrait and have my own negative for reprints." —*Michelle Craig*

Make your own cookbook as a wedding gift. "If the bride is a family member, this is a great chance to pass down family recipes, too. Here's how I did it for less than $7. I purchased a decorative photo album with four-by-six sleeves. I chose a three-ring binder ($3) so the bride could add pages. Next, I purchased some pretty recipe cards ($3.50). Finally, I pulled out my favorite recipes, copied them onto the cards, and inserted them in the sleeves. I didn't even have to fill up the album. I left blank slots at the end so the bride could insert her recipes as well." —*Crystal Smith*

"I brown bag most wedding shower gifts. Most of my friends know that is just the way Mary Nell does it. (I use leftover wallpaper to wrap a gift if I don't brown bag.)" —*Mary Nell Paris*

"I have a great idea for an unforgettable new baby gift. It will not be duplicated and will stay with the baby for life. On the day of the baby's birth, make a VCR tape of the 6:00 P.M. news. Present this to the baby's parents, and every year they can add to this on the baby's birthday. What a great way to know what went on the day of their birth. It will be a fun way to look back on headlines, hairstyles, and important events." —*Mary Beth Laster*

"For a nice but inexpensive wedding gift, take the invitation and use either De-Cal-It to make a decal or decoupage to attach the invitation to a tall candle. You can buy the candle from Wal-Mart for about $3. Then take matching ribbon (wedding color) to encircle the candle at top and bottom. It will be a keepsake to light each anniversary." —*Janet Keim*

"Find an inexpensive recipe box and fill with three-by-five index cards with family recipes. I've done this twice, for a niece and for a recently married nephew, and both times it was greatly appreciated." —*Wanda Dyer*

"Never be without gift wrapping paper again. Save the paper used to wrap merchandise—my favorite is Old Time Pottery. Press the sheets with a warm iron and roll. It is beautiful and sometimes they will give you an extra sheet." —*Minnie Swack*

"I recycle paper grocery bags when I ship gifts to family. I never buy mailing paper. If you cut the bag open at the seam and discard the bottom of the bag, you can wrap with the printing side inside. Now you have the best sturdy wrapping paper for shipping." —*Karla Cochran*

Faye Iverlett really knows how to wrap. Not only does she use the comics for the wrapping, but she makes a fanciful bow and ribbon from them as well.

Margarette Brown divides plants like aloe vera and then gives them as part of a bridal gift.

"Take a bag of chips, eat all the chips first, then turn the bag inside out. Clean the oil off the outside, then put the gift inside, and seal!" —*Sharon Brent*

"Get everyone in your family to use gift bags instead of wrapping paper for gift giving. The bags are very cheap at post-holiday sales and, being very sturdy, can be reused for years. Cheap and environmentally friendly." —*Sophia Absar*

"A good friend was moving to another state, and I wanted to do something special for her and her husband. I decided just to buy a small spiral notebook and pass it around at church and to other mutual friends and let each person take a page and write a personal note and good-bye to the couple. This worked great and was really so special to the couple who was moving. It was also a very cheap gift." —*Allison O'Dell*

"Give your time rather than purchase expensive wedding gifts. Call the mother of the bride and ask what you can do to help the wedding go more smoothly for her and the wedding party. Let her know when you will be available. I have picked up articles of clothing and wedding cakes, transported out-of-town guests, kept wedding guests overnight, made phone calls, been the caterer contact, etc. Another idea is to decorate the home with flowers from your garden." —*Barbara Wills*

 "Create a gift closet so that you will always be ready when you need birthday gifts, hostess gifts, or gifts for other events. Buy

Create a gift closet so that you will always be ready when you
need birthday gifts, hostess gifts, or gifts for other events.

items on sale and store the gifts until needed. With careful planning, you can even give out most Christmas gifts from the closet," says Barbara Stewart, whose stash includes stuffed animals, guest soaps, scented candles, bowls, and vases.

"When I am low on cash for birthday or other gifts, I take fifteen or more used CDs to Media Play. They give me a $4 store credit for each CD. I can then buy two $20 gift certificates and have $20 left in store credit to also buy a CD for myself. This way, I have shopped not only for friends but for myself as well." —*Terry Jones*

"Even when you buy an item for yourself in a shop that has free gift wrap, have them wrap it. Then carefully remove the gift wrap and use it to wrap a present to be given to another person. Usually the store gift wrap is expensive quality." —*Charlene Pippin*

"Don't throw away that deflated shiny metallic balloon. Use it to wrap a present." —*Lynn Yuchnitz*

4

Saving at the Grocery

Forty Ways to Save on Your Grocery Bill

On the cover of a recent issue of *Family Circle*, I saw a headline saying "Save $100s on Groceries." I bought the magazine (charging it to *The Tennessean* as a business expense) and started reading. The article was not exactly what I expected, but it did get me thinking. The tips were things like plan your shopping trip, compare prices, and don't assume that end-of-the-aisle displays are a bargain (often they are not).

Duh! Nothing too earth shattering. But still, I thought, if we could come up with a whole bunch of ways to save at the grocery, we could all benefit. A few pennies here, a few bucks there, and we are off to a cheaper grocery bill—which, of course, means more money for other things.

Over the years I have learned a few tricks from my own experience and from money-saving experts and readers. There are many ways to save money at the grocery. Let me count the ways:

1. Weigh all produce, not just loose products. Bags of potatoes, already packaged mushrooms, and heads of lettuce can differ in terms of weight even though they are all supposed to be the same weight and are selling at the same price. Get the one with the most in it. It's like getting free food.

2. Compare the salad bar per pound price for things like cheese, mushrooms, green peppers, and strawberries to other places in the store. This is great if you are making something that you just need a little bit of or if you are cooking up pizzas and you need a lot of little bits for toppings.

3. Look for marked-down items like holiday candy or paper goods, or torn bags of dog food or charcoal. There is usually a bin of damaged or marked-down items.

4. Buy the marked-down meat. Find out when the store routinely marks it down, and then you can stock up. Just take it home and throw it in the freezer.

5. Grate your own cheese instead of buying the already grated packages. It is almost always cheaper.

6. Make your comparisons based on price per ounce or per unit. There can be some big differences. At some stores you may need to consult your calculator, but others post unit prices on the shelf.

7. Use store brands. They are almost always cheaper, and most stores guarantee that you will like them or you can bring them back for a full refund. You have almost nothing to lose. But make sure you still compare the prices because sometimes the national brands will surprise you with special promotions and coupons.

8. Make sure you know about any discount program the store you are shopping offers—senior discount, store discount card, double coupons, free coffee, etc.

9. Don't buy chocolate milk. Just add chocolate to your milk.

10. Watch for volume discounts. You can always freeze what you don't need for later use. I buy huge packs of chicken breasts when they are on special and divide them into baggies of two each and freeze.

11. Watch for scanner errors. If the register rings up wrong at many stores, you get the item free. I have been surprised at my good luck here. But you have to really watch the register item by item and know the shelf price of the item.

12. Shop more than one store if you have time. Check various ads in the newspaper and then tailor your shopping trip (and menu) to take advantage of specials at two or even three stores.

13. Stock up when the price is right on things you know you use a lot of—things that won't spoil, like paper towels, dog food, and canned goods.

14. "Buy-one, get-one-free" can be a good deal, and many stores do not require you to actually buy two. Instead, the item just rings up half price at the register. However, I caution you to be sure that prices haven't been raised to offset the sale. The bottom line here is to know your prices.

15. Don't shop on an empty stomach. Hungry shoppers are dangerous.

16. Try to shop alone. I know that my children add dollars, dollars, dollars to the total bill, with one item here and one item there.

17. Use a list. Even if you depart from it, it helps to curb impulse buys.

Watch for volume discounts.

18. Avoid impulse buys. *Bottom Line* newsletter offers this strategy: "Whenever you take an item that is not on your shopping list, place it in the child's seat of the cart. Just before checking out, review these diet-destroying, budget-wrecking purchases. Put them all back except for one item, and consider that your reward for controlling your impulses." The booklet *Cut Your Grocery Bill in Half, Supermarket Survival* explains that if you give in and buy one bag of potato chips a week (at only $1.50), you are talking about $78 in a year. A weekly package of cookies adds up to $114 in a year. The book points out that unplanned purchases make up a third of the food items bought by 50 percent of all shoppers surveyed.

> Only a fool thinks price and value are the same.
> —Antonio Machado

I digress here to tell you a story about a friend of a friend of a friend, who was said to have shopped with her husband on Friday nights. They would go to a store, say Target or Wal-Mart, and go up and down every aisle, picking up things they would like to have. The cart would fill, but before they reached the register, they would abandon the cart and go home. I'm sure the store was furious at their lack of consideration, but you have to admit, they managed to enjoy shopping without the aftermath of bills. They never bought a thing.

19. Plan to eat what's on sale. If they have "buy-one, get-one-free" chicken breasts, it may be a good week to have chicken.

20. Plan the night meal to have enough leftover for lunches or even for another night's dinner. It sure is easier than cooking every night and can be cheaper than eating out.

21. Buy extra macaroni to add to macaroni and cheese mixes. Most packages have too much cheese anyway, so you can get two or maybe three meals from one box with some extra mac. Macaroni is cheap!

22. Make your own salad dressing and save. (But sometimes the sale prices of the prepared dressings, with coupons added, make them cheaper than preparing your own.)

23. Keep an organized pantry so that you will know what you already have.

24. Make sure that the produce you buy is fresh and that you are not buying so much that some of it may go bad before you get to it. It is easy to overbuy.

25. Shop the advertised specials and stock up.

26. Double coupon/triple coupon: Everybody knows you should coupon to save money, but if you can become more aggressive by getting friends to share coupons and by maximizing the coupon usage with already-on-sale items, you can really rack up. Make sure that you use your 55¢ and 60¢ coupons at stores that double coupons up to 60¢ instead of wasting them at stores that go only to 50¢ for doubling.

27. Use broth made from bouillon cubes instead of canned chicken broth. *Woman's Day* magazine says canned broth can cost five times as much.

28. Take advantage of free advice. Ask the butcher which cut of meat would be best for a certain recipe; ask the seafood clerk about tips for cooking fish; ask the deli clerk how long what you are buying should last.

29. Check the package sizes. Big is not always better or cheaper.

30. Ask for a rain check if an item is out of stock. Then you can come back on another shopping trip and get the advertised price.

31. Make your own marinades. Who buys this expensive stuff that you could easily make from items you already have in your pantry?

32. In the deli, ask for a sample. Most stores will gladly give you a sample of their turkey or cheese or other items. This is especially nice when you have young children with you.

33. Take advantage of the store's services. The butcher will often slice or cut or trim the meat you want and package it how you want it. Some will even season it for you. Many of the seafood counters will steam your shrimp and ice it down for you if you ask. Some also have recipe cards for different fish and ways to prepare them.

34. Buy frozen concentrated juices and add water instead of buying them already made.

35. Shop as infrequently as possible. The more you go, the more you spend. Once a week is reasonable.

36. Combine coupons with advertised specials and sometimes get items for next to nothing.

37. Look for recipes that use inexpensive ingredients.

38. Keep the purchase of convenience foods and junk foods to an absolute minimum.

39. Simplify dinners by varying the menu to include waffles or French toast, big salads, or soups and bread.

40. Make your shopping trip as quick and efficient as possible. The longer you stay, the more you spend.

Karen Buckwold offers a great strategy: "You know how we all go to the grocery and have a list but get distracted, especially if we are hungry, and end up with a cart full of stuff. Well, I play a little game with myself where I try to see how fast I can be in and out. The checkers must think I'm crazy because I will say, 'I made it in ten minutes,' or whatever. I've saved myself a lot of money."

Supermarket research shows that shoppers spend over $2 a minute after they have picked up everything they entered the store to buy. I don't know how on earth they calculated that, but you better believe I'm gonna be in a hurry from now on.

Couponing: Clip and Save

My friend Elizabeth recently confided that she had never used a coupon. My first reaction was shock, but almost immediately my thoughts turned to how I could get her to give me her unused coupons. The more I thought about it, the more intrigued I was that so many people aren't couponers. My husband is among them. I can hand him a coupon for a product he is going to the store to get, and almost inevitably, I'll find it on the floorboard of his car.

The National Promotion Marketing Association Coupon Council says less than 2 percent of the 278 billion coupons issued annually are redeemed. Why is that? "Coupon Commando" Paul Wilson says people think couponing is a hassle, they forget to take the coupons with them, they think they won't save much money, that coupons expire too fast, and they don't see coupons for the products they like. Wilson, a diehard believer in coupons, is out to prove them wrong on all accounts. He's the author of the booklet *Real Men Use Coupons Too!* and inventor of the rotary coupon file Coup-O-Dex. His studies show an annual average savings of $800 for families who regularly use coupons, and he claims to save more than $3,000 a year through aggressive couponing. Interestingly, he says that the percentage of millionaires who coupon is three times that of poverty-level shoppers.

Rule One, he says, is to shop with a list. Otherwise you become "Mr. and Mrs. Profit Margin," and spend 15 to 20 percent more than people who don't shop with a list. Wilson suggests getting your children to match up coupons to the list and split the savings.

If coupons expire too soon, Wilson says, ask to use them anyway. "Call the store and say, 'I am coming in to do a major stock-up shopping trip and I have just realized that a few of my coupons have expired. Will you accept them anyway?' The key words here are 'major stock-up shopping.' They would rather you come in and do that even if they have to accept a couple of expired coupons."

> A billion here, a billion there . . . pretty soon it adds up to real money.
> —Senator Everett Dirksen

If you think there are no coupons for the products you use, think again. Wilson suggests, "Go to your pantry and get the toll-free number off the products you like and call them and ask if they have coupons, or if they have samples or discounts. Just ask 'Where can I get coupons?' Half will send some right away, and the others will put you on their mailing lists and send you samples, T-shirts, and baseball caps. If you do this, your mailbox will be full."

Other interesting coupon facts pitched by Wilson and the council include:

- Sixty-five percent of coupons stuck on packages aren't redeemed.
- Only one percent of people surveyed said they would not use coupons no matter what.
- Based on his own couponing experiences, Wilson estimates he saves $20 to $50 an hour when he uses coupons while shopping.

Tales of Two Coupon Queens

Peggy Malone: Master of Savings

In the world of couponing, Peggy Malone is a queen. Week after week she gets the proverbial "something for nothing" by being resourceful, smart, organized, and tenacious. She has testimony after testimony (and receipts to prove it) of shopping trips on which she has gotten $160.49 worth of groceries for $5.74. Or $434.68 worth of merchandise for $72.39. She has paid $163.42 for merchandise that retails for $1,358.04. She says she comes by her ability naturally: "My mama taught me to be thrifty. She could pick more meat off a chicken than the Lord intended to put on it."

Malone works hard at couponing and rebating and tracking down bargains, spending twenty hours a week on her shopping. You see, not only does she like saving money, she's a woman on a mission. The mission is a food pantry, Master's Hands, an outreach ministry of Harvest

Christian Fellowship church, which serves as many as one hundred Nashville area families a month. Interestingly, Malone isn't even a member of the church. But boy, is she involved.

Here's how Malone's shopping mission started: Her son Guy, a member of Harvest Christian Fellowship, asked her to pick up some things for the food pantry at Thanksgiving several years ago.

"He gave me $20 and he had to help me haul it in," she says, explaining that after a few of these buying trips, she decided that if she shopped every week, she could make a big difference in the amount of food the pantry would have to give out. "I've always couponed, but I got into it big with this. I wanted to get a lot," says Malone, who is now retired after working as a waitress, bartender, in accounting, and as an office manager.

> To recommend thrift to the poor is both grotesque and insulting. It is like advising a man who is starving to eat less.
>
> —Oscar Wilde

Nowadays, Malone is the primary volunteer shopper for the pantry. She spends $20 to $30 a week, which is a combination of her own money and donations from friends, neighbors, and church members. And you wouldn't believe what she brings in for that amount because of the coupons and deals. "'Buy-one, get-one-free,' with a double coupon for each item and a rebate is my ideal," she says, laughing at how excited she gets about such savings. "And it does happen."

Malone says she was often frustrated at the grocery store when she was shopping only for herself and her husband and didn't need to buy the kind of volume where you can coupon and really save. "It left me frustrated to see all these free things on the shelf. I felt like there was someone who could use it." Now that she has a place for all of the free and cheap stuff to go, she is like a military strategist. Malone watches and waits, she organizes and plans, and when the time and price are right, she pounces.

"I can't stand to let a bargain sit there," Malone says. "When an item scans wrong, I get a rush! A lot of people don't realize that those coupons are dollar bills. Until I started doing it for Master's Hands, it was a way to save money that I enjoyed. Now I'm driven. I get anything free that can possibly be used."

> Money is your sixth sense, without which you cannot make complete use of the other five.
>
> —Somerset Maugham

And use it they do, says Master's Hands director Peggy Zide. The food pantry's rule is that it will help anybody once. "We are here for anybody who really needs food," says Zide.

"They come in and write us a grocery list," says Zide. "We do our best to see that only people who want to better their situations are able to continue receiving from us. To facilitate this, we request that they do a small act of service for us, such as emptying the trash, sweeping the floor, or replacing offering envelopes in the church chairs. We also require that they attend a Christian church. It does not have to be our church, but if it is another church, I send a letter to the pastor to inform him or her that a need exists for further assistance."

"We will help anybody if we see that they are trying," she adds. If you want to donate your leftover coupons, send them to Masters Hands, P.O. Box 328, Hermitage, TN 37076.

Peggy Malone's Secrets to Cheap Grocery Shopping

It is really a combination of all the bargain strategies that takes Peggy Malone to this high level of savings. Here are some of her "trade secrets." Obviously, shoppers in different communities will have different stores to choose from, but the principles are the same.

- Know prices. A starting point is knowing the lowest possible base price for certain items, and Malone generally uses Aldi as her base. The Aldi stores generally have vegetables for 29¢ a can. "If the coupon doesn't make it cheaper than Aldi's, I don't use it," she says.
- Shop around. In a typical week, she says she hits Kroger maybe five times, Aldi once, Sav-A-Lot once, Albertson's three times, and H. G. Hill once. She makes a trip to Dollar General and Walgreen maybe once a month, and does an occasional trip to Sam's Club. The reason for the multiple trips is mostly because of limits and because of meat markdowns, which take place almost daily.
- Travel with a cooler. This is for quality control, but also if you are shopping a lot of different stores, you don't want to have to take things home or to the pantry between stops.
- Check for scanner error. There are big savings here with many grocers giving you an item free if it rings up wrong.

- Double coupon. It is silly not to take advantage of this. Triple couponing is even better when you can get it.
- Watch the deals. Say Albertson's has bleach for 49 cents a gallon; stock up. If Sav-A-Lot has a great deal, go for it. Staples like peanut butter don't often go on sale, but when they do, if the price is better than Aldi's, stock up. Malone says the items most sought after for the pantry are peanut butter, jelly, dried beans, rice, and macaroni and cheese.
- Find coupons wherever you can. In Malone's case this is easy since congregation members bring in coupons as an additional offering to the church. She also put out a flyer in her neighborhood asking neighbors to give her their unused coupons. And Malone admits to digging through recycling bins for unused coupons. "There is good stuff there."
- Ask for rain checks. On the last day of a sale, when stores are frequently out of great-deal items, Malone goes to customer service to get rain checks, especially on items for which she has coupons.
- Rebate carefully. Malone only goes after rebates if there is something she can get free or get money back on.
- Combine strategies. For example, one of Malone's best buys was when she watched the dates on Hillshire Farm sausages and gathered coupons for them. Once they neared the expiration date and were marked down from $1.79 to $.99, she whipped out her $.55 double coupons and got them for nothing and slapped them in the freezer. She did the same thing with boneless chicken tenders, combining the sale price, markdown, and senior coupons to get multiple packages at $.25 a pound.

Coupon Facts

- Almost 83 percent of households in North America use coupons at least sometimes; 77 percent of men and 88 percent of women use coupons
- In 1999 6.5 billion supermarket coupons were redeemed, which represents only 3 percent of all coupons distributed in the year.
- The average value of a coupon redeemed in 1999 was 72¢.
- Using six average coupons a week in 1999 equated to $225 in annual savings.

Sources: *Real Men Use Coupons, Too* by Paul A. Wilson and International Data.

Coupon Queen, Freddie Walker

Over the years as Ms. Cheap, I have run into some pretty impressive and aggressive couponers—people who have saved $150 with triple coupons, people who have stockpiled the money they saved with coupons and used it for exotic trips or grandchildren's education, people who plan their entire food lives around coupons. Few come close to Freddie Walker, the undeniable coupon queen of Mount Pleasant, Tennessee.

By her calculations, Walker has managed to buy $1,000 worth of groceries for $99 using her clever and savvy couponing techniques. And a visit to her three-bedroom home is testimony enough. The home is neat and tidy, but you can bet your bottom dollar that there is coupon-pur-chased stuff stashed everywhere—dozens of brand-new tubes of tooth-paste under the bed, canned green beans in a drawer ("my husband likes green beans"), cake mixes, confectioners' sugar, and boxes of rice in the closet. And the attic is loaded with boxes of paper towels, garbage bags, oven bags, shampoos, barbecue sauce, and chili. It's all name-brand stuff, and you can also bet that Walker got most of it for almost nothing.

> A dollar saved is worth a whole lot more than a dollar earned.
>
> —Freddie Walker

"This is my job. This is my lifestyle," says Walker, a forty-six-year-old mother of two almost-grown children. "They call me Mr. Haney, you know, from *Green Acres*, the one who has everything."

Her grocery receipts bear out her couponing savvy—$39.11 worth of groceries for $5.87, $20.23 worth of groceries for $3.36, $9.45 worth of groceries for $1.43. Just to give you an idea of what she got, the $1.43 bought five bottles of Wylie's Beef Bouillon cubes, two packs of beef stew mix, and two boxes of oven bags. The bouillon cubes alone would have been $1.19 each at the regular price.

When told of Walker's phenomenal coupon savings, Kroger regional spokesman Ross Thomas said, "Good for her! We hear stories of people who are really saving with coupons. She must be really good at it." Walker shops mostly at the Kroger in Columbia, Tennessee, but also drops in other stores like the Bi-Lo for other specials, like the day she bought twenty-four cans of Del Monte green beans with double coupons and a Bi-Lo bonus card for almost nothing.

"The green beans were originally 63¢ a can, but my bonus card took 30¢ off each can, making them 33¢ a can. And then I had a coupon that gave $1 off on four cans. I think I got them for 14¢ a can," she said proudly. "Just the other day I got ten boxes of tea bags for 30¢ at Bi-Lo. They were on sale, and I had my card and coupons!"

Walker was the younger of two children raised by a blind mother, who instilled in her the work ethic and a sense of value and quality. "She taught us to buy quality but not to pay a lot of money for it. I grew up with rich tastes but no money," Walker said with a laugh.

Walker and her husband, Wendell, have been married for twenty-six years and have two children, in whom they are trying to instill the same kind of values. Wendell is a factory worker and so was Freddie until several years ago when she was injured in two automobile accidents, which left her disabled with degenerative disk disease and unable to return to the traditional work force. That is when she took on couponing as a serious vocation.

"We were really suffering income-wise," she said, explaining that in addition to her overwhelming medical bills, her daughter had two brain surgeries and her husband's job was downsized to a lower paying position. "It all hit at once," she said. "We had to restructure our finances. I was already frugal. We didn't have credit cards or any of that, thank goodness, but we were struggling and I was feeling like I was not contributing much to the family income. I planned out a budget and started

> Those who have little, if they are good at managing, must be accounted among the rich.
>
> —Socrates

looking at where I could cut costs. I started couponing to a higher volume. I realized that a penny saved is more than a penny earned. It is tax-free money. I tried to explain that to my husband, and I announced that I was going to get $1,000 worth of groceries for $99. A lot of people said, 'you can't do it,' but a lot of others said, 'how can we help?'"

Her big break came when her grocery, Kroger, announced its first-ever triple coupons on coupons up to 50¢. "This was a dream," Walker said. "I got my kids from Sunday school to help me sort coupons. I got hot dogs and drinks—with coupons, of course—and they kept on working."

Walker went to Kroger and got $121 worth of groceries for $18. "I calculated it and said, 'I've got to do better than that.'" She cashed in on rebates. She looked for specials. She asked people for their coupons. "I check the Sunday paper like some people do the Dow Jones," she said.

> Accumulating debt is exactly like eating too much fat and suffering the consequences.
> —Ginger Applegarth, from *The Money Diet*

Asked to give details of her very best deal, she said, "One day I went to Kroger during triple coupons, and I had 50¢-off coupons for tuna. The tuna was $1.49, so I got it free, forty cans of tuna. And then when I went through the checkout, I got a bonus coupon for $1 off on my next trip." Another time she got five bottles of Tropicana orange juice free because of a scanner error in which the item rang up wrong. Walker admits that she buys things she cannot use, but comes back with the fact that she never buys anything that someone else can't use.

Harvey Slate, with the Association of Coupon Professionals, said he was not surprised by Walker's hefty savings. "We've heard of these kinds of things, especially if the shopping list is geared to the coupons. The savings are definitely there. In 1999 consumers saved more than $3 billion using coupons."

But for Walker, the couponing is a mission, not just a challenge. "By doing this, I was able to bless so many other people. I like to give gifts. If I can get it free, I can pass it on. I fill baskets with things I get with coupons." She creates gift baskets for weddings, birthdays, housewarmings, graduations, even for a friend's bad hair day.

Tricks of the Trade

How does Freddie Walker manage to get so much for so little? She says it is a combination of things:

- Use multiple coupons. "Friends and relatives from all over the country send me the coupons they are not using. I get coupons anywhere I can get them. I even get them out of the garbage. I ask for them; I tell people, 'give me your inserts,'" says Walker.
- Stay organized. Walker keeps her coupons organized so that when she goes shopping, she doesn't miss anything. She organizes them by category—household cleaners, cereal, meat, spices, paper goods, soap, and so on.
- Watch the checker. Make sure all coupons are scanned through.

- Plan your menus. Use coupons to plan meals.
- Get serious. View saving money and couponing as a job and really work at it.
- Barter. Walker has been known to trade her "freebies" for other things she needs—clothes, hairstyling, nails, and more. She says, "One time I traded baked beans for two hundred people for a suit, a pretty suit. I barter with what I have."
- Think "no limits." Walker comments, "It is not just groceries, I use coupons for everything—hotels, medication. When we travel, we stay in luxurious hotels for as little as $49. I'm not talking about Motel 6. I'm talking about places like Embassy Suites. I have coupons with me everywhere I go."

What she doesn't use, she donates to charity or her church, the Dry Fork Church of Christ. "I like to share. If you have your fist closed, can't anything come to you."

Tips: Grocery Shopping

"Start a coupon club at your work or within your neighborhood. Clip the coupons that you will use and then take your leftovers and share." —*Victoria Hunt*

"The first day of a 'buy-one, get-one-free' sale, buy one or two and get your freebies. Then on the last day of the sale, go back; there's a good chance these items will be gone. Then get a rain check made out for sev-

eral of them. This way you have the freebies over a long period of time."
—*Marie Jett*

"Always save your grocery receipts and never fail to look for errors.
Just this week I was charged twice for the same item." —*Fay Thompson*

"Whenever possible, save your coupons until the item goes on sale—
that way your savings multiplies." —*Victoria Hunt*

Health food stores that sell items in bulk are the best place to shop for
spices, herbs, baking yeast, soy sauce, vanilla, and so on. "The items are
only a fraction of the price of the prepackaged items." —*Eunice Doty*

We are all duped by paper products because most are pumped up
with air to make them look bigger and none of them have product
weight information on the packaging. "It is impossible to compare the
actual paper content of paper goods from information on the package.
How do you do it? You take two or three packages of toilet paper or
paper towels to the produce section and weigh them. With a pocket
calculator you can quickly figure cost per pound and the actual best
buy." —*Bill Wills*

"Here is what I believe could save quite a sum over a year's time:
Most people have x amount of money in the budget for food. Well, if
a person goes to the grocery store on Friday one week, on Saturday
the next, and Sunday the next week, and so on, in seven weeks the

store is visited six times, saving one week's grocery bill every seven weeks (hope you can understand this)." —*Billy Fiveash*

"Only cut out coupons of articles that you will buy. If you cut more, then you will end up buying frivolous items that you normally would not buy." —*Patty Beazley*

Don't miss any scanner error possibilities. "I always have a list. When I pick up any item, I write down the shelf price beside where it is on my list. This way, I have the price right with me, in case I think I have been overcharged. Albertson's and Kroger will give you the item free if you have been overcharged. Wal-Mart gives the item free up to $3 or takes off $3 if the price is over that." —*Lynn Yuchnitz*

"When standing in line waiting to check out at the grocery, pick up a magazine to look at. You'll have time to read a couple of articles or recipes, and it will calm your nerves and make the wait pleasurable instead of aggravating." —*Lillian Harrell*

5

Saving at Home

Saving money and being frugal is nothing new. A little book called *1003 Household Hints and Work Savers* was put out in 1959 by Third National Bank (now part of the banking giant SunTrust) and it is a doozie. I was happy to see that saving money and being frugal was "in" even then. But indeed times have changed. I have had a ball going through the book and finding advice that still applies and some that made me laugh out loud. I'll share some of both. (You decide which is which.)

- Before putting woolen bathing suits away, wash to discourage moths; dry thoroughly; store in paper wrapping, sealed so that it is airtight.
- A fur should not be hung in a closet while wet, nor placed near a heated radiator. Precaution: Shake the fur till the top hairs fluff, then hang in an open place. Also, as much as possible, keep furs away from strong sunlight.

- It pays to do your clothes buying with laundering in mind. Buy fabrics that wash easily, dry quickly, and need little or no ironing.
- To judge the quality of woolen material, squeeze it in your hand. It should feel smooth, rubbery, springy when you open your hand. If it has a rough feeling, the grade is inferior.
- If you drive a car, get in on the side nearest the wheel instead of scraping along the whole seat until you worm your way into position, thus causing more wear on your clothes, especially furs.
- Keep your sweaters shapely by following these rules: (1) Never overload sweater pockets so they sag out of shape; (2) Never put sweaters on hangers. Between wearings fold them neatly and lay them in a drawer; (3) Before washing a sweater, sew the button holes together so they will not stretch out of shape. That is what is meant by the "stitch in time."
- For longest hosiery wear, the right stocking length is important. Be sure to choose the proper length for your own proportions. Hose too long must be fastened below the welt (double top part), causing runs. Hose too short will develop breaks and runs when the knee is bent. A good rule of thumb is for anyone with larger thighs to buy stockings so that the welt will come just below the widest part of the leg when you are seated.
- Here's how to hang clothes so they will not stretch out of shape or be disfigured by pin marks. Hang men's shirts by folding the bottom three or four inches of the tail over the line and pin at ends. Fold sheets hem-to-hem and turn about four inches over the line. Use one clothespin at either end and two in the middle to prevent

sagging. Make sure the sheet hangs straight. Fold handkerchiefs over the line. Don't let them hang by one end. Never hang any garments by the shoulders.

• Never do your housework in a trailing housecoat and mules. Such apparel will not only tire you, but it is dangerous. You may trip over them or catch your sleeves on pot handles.

• Rid rooms of stale tobacco smoke with your own homemade deodorizer. Just mix a little diluted ammonia with a bowl of fresh water and let the bowl stay overnight in the room to be purged. Try this in your clothes closets too.

• Wicker furniture should be cleaned by scrubbing with a stiff brush moistened with warm salt water. Salt keeps the wicker from turning yellow.

• To brighten a rug, sprinkle salt over it before using the vacuum cleaner. Sweeps out the soot.

• You'll prevent the inside of your salt shaker metal top from rusting if you paint it with ordinary nail polish. When the lacquer is dry, use a darning needle to open the holes from the inside out.

• A tremendous time and wear saver for home laundering is the automatic dryer. There's no worry about changing weather, no lifting of heavy wet clothes up basement steps to hang on an outside line, no scurrying out to the yard or up to the roof to remove flapping clothes if it storms suddenly. The dryer also saves much ironing. Articles such as Turkish towels, bedspreads, corduroy play clothes, most underwear, and cotton rugs need only be fluff dried, taken out, and stored.

- Brassieres are easy to iron. Iron toward the center of each cup, turning the brassiere on the board until each area is smooth and dry. Then iron the flat sections and the straps.
- Government studies show that Americans waste fully 20 percent of their food through spoilage and over-generous portions. Serve moderate helpings first, second helpings if wanted. This sensible practice minimizes unusable leftovers, and moderate helpings look more appetizing. For every $10 you spend on food each week, you can save approximately $2 according to the government, merely by adopting this highly rewarding habit.
- Use up that bit of leftover meat by combining it in a cream sauce and serving it piping hot with toasted corn bread squares or by grinding together with minced vegetables and mixing with mayonnaise for tasty, nutritional spreads.
- Don't buy a quart of sour milk or buttermilk because you need a cupful for a recipe. Just add two tablespoons of vinegar to one cup of sweet milk and stir. Presto. Sour milk!
- A little oatmeal adds much flavor and richness when used as a thickener for soups. Try it.
- Desalt that over-salted soup by merely slicing a raw potato into it and boiling for a short time. Then remove the potato, which will have absorbed most of the salt.
- Place a piece of apple in your brown sugar jar and it will keep the sugar from drying out and lumping. Try the same cure for too dry cookies.
- Who's too proud for day-old bread? It's not only cheaper and just

as nourishing, but actually better for the teeth and gums, according to experts. Did you know that day-old bread makes better toast than fresh bread?

- Rolls and muffins that have hardened to the "can't be et" stage are easily freshened. Sprinkle the rolls with water, place in a brown paper bag, and warm in a hot oven for a few moments.
- When that sub deb outgrows her slacks, bring them back alive with this fine fashion trick. Add trouser borders of knitted yarn and sew a matching knitted band around the waist.
- An umbrella frame stripped of its cover makes a good rack on which to dry small articles such as hankies, gloves, etc. To avoid the danger of rust, first spread a clean white cloth over the frame.
- When dusting, don't overlook the light bulbs. So many housewives fail to realize that a two-second swipe with a cloth over a dusty bulb can increase your light by as much as 50 percent.
- When making long distance telephone calls, place an hourglass egg-timer near your telephone. It operates on a three-minute schedule and will warn you when your three minutes are up.
- Halving your large potatoes before baking them will lessen fuel consumption.
- Always remove cellophane wrapping from a new lampshade before using it. Heat and atmospheric conditions cause it to warp and wrinkle in the shade.
- To stuff feathers in a pillow quickly and neatly, substitute the ticking for the vacuum cleaner bag. Dump the feathers on paper, turn on the vacuum, and draw them in.

- It's good psychology to keep a box of facial tissues in the bathroom when having guests. Most women will thoughtfully use these instead of guest towels to remove excess lipstick.
- Chill candles in the refrigerator for twenty-four hours before using them on the table. They will burn evenly and will not drip.
- If you enjoy gardening but want to avoid grimy fingernails, scrape them over a wet cake of soap before beginning to work. This will keep the dirt out and the soap will easily rinse out afterward.
- Chimney soot makes fine fertilizer for gardens and potted plants. Cold tea also makes fine fertilizer for house plants and acts as an insecticide as well.

Cheap Cleaners

I love spring, but I have to admit I have a hard time getting enthused about the spring-cleaning part of it. I tried to figure out just what it was I didn't like and decided that it boiled down to two things: One, cleaning is hard work; and two, it can be expensive if you buy a lot of these commercial cleaners that make it look easier. It's gotten to the point where there's a special product for cleaning every little thing—cleaners for kitchens, ovens, bathrooms, outdoor windows, indoor windows, countertops, bathtubs, cabinets, showers, and on and on.

It would be so much better if you could make your own cleaner that would work for everything, or at least if you could make a few cheap

> There is a use for almost everything.
>
> —George Washington Carver

cleaners from a few basic ingredients and get on with it. The basic ingredients like ammonia, borax, bleach, vinegar, and baking soda are pretty
cheap, after all. (Remember, though, never mix ammonia and bleach
together! It creates toxic fumes.)

Over the years as Ms. Cheap, I've read (and printed) a lot of recipes
for cleaners, both from clever readers and from other cheap publica-
tions. Here you go:

- *All-purpose cleaner 1:* Mix ½ cup of ammonia, ½ cup of vinegar, and
  ¼ cup of baking soda into 1 gallon of warm water. —*Cheapskate
  Monthly*
- *All-purpose cleaner 2:* In 1 quart of warm water, mix 1 teaspoon
  each of liquid soap, boric acid (borax), and lemon juice and/or
  vinegar. —*A Penny Saved* newsletter
- *All-purpose cleaner 3:* Mix ½ cup of ammonia, ⅓ cup of vinegar, 2
  tablespoons of baking soda, and 1 gallon of water. —*Tightwad
  Gazette*
- *Abrasive cleaner:* "Dip lemon half in borax. Scrub surface. Rinse
  well." —*A Penny Saved*
- *Disinfectant:* Mix ½ cup of borax in 1 gallon of water. —*A Penny
  Saved*
- *Disinfectant spray:* "In a spray bottle, mix ½ cup of chlorine bleach
  with 3½ cups of water. Costs about a dime versus $5 for a name-
  brand spray." —*Cheap Tricks*
- *Tile cleaner:* Mix ¼ cup of vinegar with 1 gallon of water. "It doesn't
  leave a film and removes dirt without scrubbing." —Eva Hollis

It would be so much better if you could make your
own cleaner that would work for everything.

- *Soap scum remover:* To clean hardened soap scum on tiles, "coat the entire surface with undiluted liquid detergent and allow it to dry overnight. Wet the surface and scrub with a stiff brush and scouring powder. Rinse and buff with a bath towel." —*Bottom Line*
- *Mildew remover 1:* Mix equal parts of bleach and water. Spray on mildew. When stains are gone, rinse really well. —Kitty Walker
- *Mildew remover 2:* "Use full-strength vinegar to wipe soap film and mildew from shower curtains and tile." —Patricia Rickman
- *Showerhead cleaner:* "Pour 1 cup of vinegar in a plastic bag, secure bag to shower head. Let stand overnight, rinse." —*A Penny Saved*
- *Toilet bowl cleaner 1:* "Sprinkle baking soda in the bowl, drizzle with vinegar, and then scrub with a brush." —*Cheapskate Monthly.*
- *Toilet bowl cleaner 2:* "Pour used denture solution in toilet. Let sit." —*A Penny Saved*
- *Glass and window cleaner:* "Put club soda in a spray bottle for a very simple glass cleaner, or mix ½ cup of vinegar and ½ cup of water in a spray bottle." —*Cheapskate Monthly*
- *Window cleaner:* Mix ¼ cup of ammonia and 1 quart of water. "Terrific and huge savings." —Kitty Walker
- *Wall cleaner:* Mix 1 gallon of hot water with ½ cup of borax. —*Miserly Moms*
- *Rust remover:* "Salt will get rid of rust. A peeled potato dipped in baking soda or salt works great to remove rust from almost any surface." —Connie Crowell
- *Furniture polish:* Mix 1 part lemon juice with 2 parts vegetable or olive oil. — *Miserly Moms*

- *Stain pre-treater:* Mix equal parts of ammonia, liquid dishwasher detergent, and water. Put in an empty dishwashing liquid bottle. Shake well. "I just love this because it works as well as Spray 'N' Wash for much less money." —Kitty Walker
- *Stain remover:* Mix 1 cup of Clorox 2 color safe bleach, 1 cup of Cascade dishwasher powder, and a few gallons of hot water in a 5-gallon bucket. The water must be very, very hot. Soak the stained garment overnight and then wash as you regularly would. "It almost always works, but you have to be sure that the Cascade is completely dissolved." —Corinne Sandifer
- *Grease remover:* Combine dishwasher liquid, vinegar, and corn-meal. This is a good cleaner for anyone who works on cars or lawnmowers; it really cuts the black oil or grease. —Pam Barber
- *Carpet deodorizer:* "Mix together, in container with tight-fitting lid, 2 cups of baking soda, ½ cup of cornstarch, 5 crumbled bay leaves, and 1 tablespoon of ground cloves. Shake container well, sprinkle liberally over carpet. Vacuum fully." —A Penny Saved
- *Carpet cleaner 1:* Use Sprite soda to remove dirt spots from your carpet. Pour enough to soak, and then pat dry with a rag. —Kristi Petty
- *Carpet cleaner 2:* "To remove a food stain or pet stain from carpet and furniture, pour a small amount of white vinegar on the spot. Rub until the area is wet and then use a dry rag to get it as dry as possible." —Jill Stout

I've also received some interesting suggestions for handling hard-to-clean items:

- *Window screens:* "Run dry nylon scrubbies over the screens and the dirt will fly out." —*A Penny Saved*
- *Shower curtain:* "Wash in washing machine with towels, detergent, and one cup of white vinegar mixed in with the water. Remove before the final spin; hang on rod." —*A Penny Saved*
- *Scratched furniture or picture frames:* "Use a walnut hull (wear gloves) and rub hull on scratch. You can also use walnut hulls on baskets to stain them to give them an old look." —Helen Coker
- *Pleated lampshades:* "Clean with a baby's hairbrush." —*A Penny Saved*
- *Wallpaper:* "Rub with soft chunks of white bread" and finger marks and stains will come off. —*A Penny Saved* (I wonder what would happen if you used whole wheat bread!)
- *Brass:* Paint tomato catsup on your brass and copper lamps and other objects. Let set for several hours. Remove with hot soapy water. —Kathryn Groover

I haven't tried all of these, but I trust my readers and these cheap-cleaning experts—even the tomato catsup on the brass idea. Catsup isn't cheap, but it surely sounds a lot better than buying umpteen products for cleaning and shining, especially if it works.

P.S. Be sure to label any cleaners you make up so that you know what you have for future use and of course keep them out of the reach of children and pets.

Tips: Cleaning

Bathroom cleaners with scrubbing bubbles can clean almost anything, says Cindy Huff, who uses it to clean doors, walls, appliances, window sills, sneakers, linoleum floors, screen doors, spots in her car, and of course, the bathroom.

Alice Huang made her own duster out of dryer sheets, a chopstick, and a rubber band. Her instructions: "Fold about ten pieces of fabric softener sheets over and tie them to the chopstick. If you want something longer for higher spots, use a longer stick."

"Instead of vacuuming the fringe on rugs, use a comb or hair lifter to straighten the fringe. The vacuum cleaner is too hard on it, and over time a lot of fringe would be lost." —*Margaret Jones*

"When motor oil was spilled on the garage floor, it was a mess. I sprinkled baking soda all over the oil spot, let it set for five minutes, and then swept it up. All the oil was gone." —*Sue Garrett*

"I keep the little perfume samples that come in magazines and tape them to the ceiling fan to freshen a room." —*Ramona Kaiser*

"To freshen up a room fast, use baby powder or your favorite scented body powder. Sprinkle it on the carpet, wait a few minutes, take a broom and gently brush into the carpet, and vacuum. It leaves the room smelling clean and fresh." —*Darlene Fuller*

"For water spots on the table, cover the spot with mayo, petroleum jelly, or butter overnight. For tougher water stains, use toothpaste. For even tougher water spots, use toothpaste and some baking soda." —*Lynn Yuchnitz*

"A used dryer sheet works great for cleaning soap scum from your bathroom sink. Rub briskly and your sink will shine. Use dryer sheets to clean the mirror too." —*Maxene Celsor*

Connie Wynn says she keeps the newspapers she has already read and uses them to clean glass and mirrors.

White Out (liquid paper) can help with spots on everything from clothing to carpeting. "Care has to be taken as to what shade of white is involved, and one needs to 'feather it out.'" —*Carmen Pearson*

Saving Water

Saving water is a necessity during a drought, but it can help you save money rain or shine. That's why I'm showering you with these tips from Helen Bussell of Brentwood, Tennessee, who learned about water savings when she lived in California.

- Don't flush the toilet every time.
- Don't let water run while you're brushing your teeth or washing dishes.

- Don't run the dishwasher or washing machine unless it is full. Use the dishwasher's water miser or short cycle setting if possible.
- If you take a tub bath, use one to two inches less water. If you shower, take two to three minutes less time. Also use a bucket in the shower to catch the water as you wait for it to heat up. Use this water on your plants.
- If you use yard sprinklers, make sure they're working and aimed properly. Don't water the concrete. Check for leaks or drips. Don't dump water down the drain. Find out how to use it twice.
- If you have a bird bath, keep the water fresh and clean for the animals who need it. Use old water for plants and shrubs.
- During a drought, "do a rain dance. You never know. It might help!" says Bussell.

Tips: Saving Water

"When I wash clothes, my husband catches a bucket of the soapy water when it pumps out and mops the floor with it. Sure cuts down on our water bill." —Andrea Parsons

Eighty-four-year-old Paul Rhea lines up five-gallon buckets along the edge of his carport and catches enough rainwater to water his wife's pretty flowers all summer long. After every sizable rain, he just transfers the collected rainwater to gallon jugs and he is all set.

The national vice is waste.
—Henry Miller

Tips: Saving in the Bathroom and on Beauty Products

Julie Parker suggested the "TP Crunch." "By stepping on a roll of toilet paper and causing the roll to 'crease,' one can keep the paper from rolling freely, thus decreasing the amount to come off per roll."

Patricia Martin uses a strategically placed paper clip to guarantee that she squeezes every last bit from the toothpaste tube.

"When I open a bottle of vitamins or aspirin, I always save the cotton stuffed in the top. It is good quality. I just pinch off the amount of cotton I need for manicures, etc." —*Mary Ann Liden*

"I take leftover slivers of soap and put them in a quart jar. I add boiling water and let stand. After a short time, I mix up softened soap and water. I use Soft Soap containers (that I bought with coupons) and use a funnel to fill them with the soapy mixture." —*Barbara Walther*

"To make a nail polish remover container, put a sponge roller in a film canister and fill with liquid remover." —*Lynn Yuchnitz*

"An inexpensive and effective way to remove face and eye makeup is to use alcohol-free baby wipes. Buy the store-brand ones in the square containers and then buy the refill packs and refill. Baby wipes are also great for removing makeup stains from clothes. But I suggest that you test the fabric first." —*Mary Roberts*

"When I want to pamper myself but not spend a lot of money, I go to a beauty school and treat myself to an eyebrow wax or manicure. All of their services are inexpensive, yet I feel like I have treated myself to a splurge." —*Joy Wells*

"Being a makeup freak, I have tried many that did not work—too thin, too thick, too red, or too yellow. I used to toss these things out. Finally, I got smart and cheap and started mixing the different brands, colors, and consistencies until I had the perfect makeup for my complexion. Doing this, I have saved a lot of money and had fun mixing and getting the best makeup I have ever worn." —*Jean Caillouette*

"Take a citrus bag that lemons come in and use it for a cosmetic bag in your purse. All the cosmetics are kept together, and you can see just what you need." —*Vi Prosser*

"I (also my husband and children) go to a local beauty school to have my hair cut, colored, and styled. It costs me $22 every five to six weeks; a friend of mine pays $60 for the same service at a local beauty shop." —*Donna King*

"I save my too-small pieces of soap by inserting them in a loofah (dish rag gourd). They lather like crazy. I use them for bathing my body or scrubbing appliances." —*Judy Harvey*

"Often a department store cosmetic promotion includes a lipstick that

When I want to pamper myself but not spend
a lot of money, I go to a beauty school.

may not be a favorite shade. I use it as a base coat with my favorite shade as a top coat, thereby making it last twice as long." —*Agnes Wells*

"Don't throw away your lipstick when it gets down to the edge of the tube. Take the tip of a skinny makeup brush and dig a small amount of the lipstick onto it and apply to your lips. You would be surprised at how many more times you can use it before it is down to its last smear." —*Carol Bohrman*

"Prop near-empty roll-on deodorant, shampoo, lotion, etc., facedown in a suitable size cup. You will get an extra week or so out of the item." —*Carole Barenys*

"Use plain old witch hazel for a less harsh, very effective astringent for your face. At about 68¢ a bottle, it serves the same purpose as Clinique's pricey astringents. You can even fill an old Clinique bottle if vanity is the issue. Also use baby oil to remove eye makeup. It's cheap and irritant free and softens your skin at the same time." —*Nancy Ledford*

"When emptying a plastic container that held lotion or shampoo, etc., I cut the container in half so I can scrape the remaining lotion or whatever out." —*JoAnn Rogers*

"When nail polish begins to get thick, one or two drops of remover extends its life considerably." —*Corinne Ford*

"Use toilet tissue instead of Kleenex to blow your nose." —*Bill Turner*

"I purchase a small can of Crisco shortening and empty it into a mixing bowl. I add a drop or two of red food coloring, three or four squirts of a favorite fragrance, and a tablespoon of water. I then beat with the electric mixer for a few minutes. The texture becomes very light and fluffy. I spoon it into an attractive tin or container and use it as I would any cleanser to remove makeup. My skin is slightly dry, so after cleansing, I smooth a little over my face as a night moisturizer. This also works extremely well for dry hands, elbows, feet, and so on. I've even given it as gifts to friends. They love it!" —*Faye Iverlett*

Robert Anderson says he saves on the light bill by unscrewing two of the four bulbs in his vanity light, using only two at a time: "The two remaining lights give off more than enough light, and when a bulb burns out, I simply swap it with the unused bulb."

"I love the feel and smell of perfumed body powder but hate to pay the expensive price for it. I take a clean cottage cheese carton and fill it about half full with pure cornstarch. I spray several sprays of my favorite fragrance, close tightly, shake well, and, voilà, I have a great smelling dusting powder." —*Jessie Cobb*

"A discarded toothbrush makes an excellent nail brush." —*Mary Ann French*

"Free odor remover and eyebrow liner. Save freebie matchbooks. Light one, wave it around briefly to get rid of odors. Sulfur in the match does the trick. Dampen the tip and break it off. It works perfectly as an eyebrow liner!" —Carmel Redmon

"I use worn panty hose as a ponytail holder and as rubber bands. Simply cut panty hose into three-inch-wide pieces and use as a ponytail holder." —Yvonne Brewington

"When bar soap has gotten too small to use, you can put a rubber band around two or three of the small pieces and create a new bar." —Corinne Ford

"When you have used the last drop of hand cream (or other products) that you can squeeze out, cut off the bottom of the tube and you will have another week or so left. Just stand the tube on its lid when not in use." —Fran Allen

"Use inexpensive shaving cream to clean your face. It has oil and will not dry your skin. I've used this for years." —Kathryn Groover

"Olive oil is an effective and economical beauty aid. Use as a nighttime moisturizer. It maintains the elasticity of the skin and prevents wrinkles. Olive oil can prevent stretch marks during pregnancy. Simply smooth on the abdomen nightly during pregnancy. Make a paste with olive oil and salt and use as an exfoliant. A few drops of an essential oil such as lavender can be added to enhance its soothing effects." —Donna Davis

Vikki Harris says to make great-smelling lotion, she buys the cheap dollar-store kind and adds four or five drops of her favorite scent (Red Door) to it. "It's great!"

"I don't buy colognes. I tear out all the advertised pages with the scents for men and women from the magazines at my doctor's office. *Cosmopolitan* is the best." —*Margaret Martin*

" If you can't cut your own hair, at least try a discount chain. Most hair stylists get the same amount of training. Learn to color your own hair if you color. A $5 dye kit will have the same results as a $55 salon visit if you learn how to do it right." —*Mary Carter*

"Save 50 percent on shampoo. Most shampoo labels say to shampoo a head twice. One good shampoo works just as well." —*Pat Helm*

Tips: Decorating on the Cheap

Pam Barber says that instead of purchasing expensive mat board for picture frames, she uses colored poster board.

"Having built a new home, I needed to watch my decorating budget. In the guest bedroom, instead of buying a wooden pole for a curtain rod, I saved money by sawing off the end of a broomstick to the necessary length. I sprayed two small plastic pineapples gold and then wiped them with antique stain, attaching the pineapples to the broomsticks as finials." —*Corinne Wright*

"Take all of your old and mismatched white, light, and dingy sheets—even printed linen with a light background—select a pleasing color RIT liquid dye, and color them. Then enjoy your new and elegantly matched bedroom." —*Virginia Studer*

"You can have carpet remnants bound as rugs for less than the price of a new rug. So if you are taking up the carpet from your bedroom, use the piece under the bed to make a rug." —*the "Cheap Creep"*

Don't throw away worn throw pillows. Just "buy remnants of decor-matching material and cut to the size of the old pillows. Instead of stuffing with new fiber fill, I simply use the old pillows." —*Phyllis Herman*

"For inexpensive napkin rings, use shower hooks ($1 for a box of ten) and glue silk flowers or other decorations to them. They are sold in a variety of colors to match table decorations." —*Janet Keim*

"I buy those big three-wick candles on sale and then burn only one wick at a time." —*Diane Wiles*

"Save the flip-tops from your aluminum cans. They can be glued on the back of almost anything and used as a hanger. They can even be sewn on the backs of small wall hangings." —*Opel Smith*

"Curtain rods and hardware are so expensive. Instead, we used fence post tops (finials), which came with a large screw in the bottom anyway.

We painted some decoratively, others just plain white, screwed them in the wall above our windows, and swagged fabric over the knobs for a quick and pretty window treatment." —*Kim Borum*

Barbara Wills transformed her dining room into a Florida room very economically and creatively using plants, an outdoor table, and matching chairs instead of buying an expensive dining room suite.

Ruth Dean wanted two round neck pillows, but in stores they were $30 to $35 each. "I bought two cheap rolls of paper towels, then went to a fabric outlet and bought material and matching ribbon. I covered each roll of towels in the fabric, taping the cloth edge to the towels, and ending with the selvage outside. I then tied the ribbon in bows at each end. They are quite lovely and cost me less than $10."

> Never spend your money before you have it.
> —Thomas Jefferson

"Use shower curtain rods instead of expensive wood or brass rods when hanging tab top curtains or valances. Then set the rods on planter hooks like you would use to hang plant baskets from the wall. Rod and hooks come in many colors and for one window would cost less than $10." —*Leigh Hamilton*

"For free decor for a dorm room or first apartment, try maps. Most state tourism departments have toll-free numbers where you can call to request free maps and brochures. Wyoming is my favorite." —*Sara Woodall*

"Use scarves for table runners."
—J. C. Matthews

Barbara Stewart buys colorful vintage tablecloths and uses them as accent pieces on a table, as curtains, and even as throws on the backs of chairs.

Melinda Hamilton bought plates for a quarter at Goodwill, then took them home, broke them, and glued the pieces down to make a "beautiful counter top."

"I save my small pieces of soap and melt them down to make liquid hand soap." —Mary Bancroft

"If you like a certain scent of perfume or cologne, but it is too expensive, try finding a bottle of bath oil of that scent. It is usually a fraction of the price and lasts a long time. Also it does not evaporate. Just be careful not to stain clothes with it." —M. L. Samies

Tips: Gardening

"Before planting a garden, have your soil tested by your county agricultural extension service. That way you will know what to add for the best crop results." —Bob Battle

"Buy perennial plants at the end of the season even if they are almost dead. Give them a little TLC and water, and the following spring they will do well." —*Lisa Kersey*

"To kill weeds and grass, especially between bricks in the sidewalk or patio, buy one gallon of bleach for 79¢, punch five or six nail holes in the lid to make a sprinkler, and soak the undesirables. In a couple of hot days, all dead!" —*Ida F. Payne*

"Use newspapers as mulch. Place them around plants and cover with a thin layer of soil and grass clippings to keep them from blowing away. Mulching saves on water use, so you save on mulch and water." —*Linda Dixon*

"Use plastic tops from coffee cans, ice cream, or other containers for water trays under flowers instead of buying the trays." —*June Andree*

Julie Berbiglia shared this recipe for free liquid plant food: "Use a handful of finished compost, put it in an old panty-hose leg, and tie shut to make a 'tea bag.' Soak twenty-four hours in a bucket with one to two gallons of water. Dilute it with more water until it is the color of weak tea. Use as a foliar spray on houseplants and to feed vegetable seedlings."

"A great money saver in the flower beds is to help the neighbors clean weeds and debris from their garden in the spring. As 'payment,' request the opportunity to separate some of the items or even remove some to be planted in your garden. It helps them and offers you new color and texture for your flower beds." —*Christopher Taylor*

"Drives in the country can offer beauty to take back to your home if you take a trowel, clippers, baggies, and water containers" and dig up some roadside plants. —*Judy Parks*

"I plant several beds of zinnia flower seeds every spring. They begin blooming in early summer and bloom through first frost. They make great cut flowers, so I have fresh flowers in the house all summer and fall." — *Daryl Brown*

Joyce Hughey says, "The next time you receive or buy a floral arrangement from a grocery or florist, save the white and purple (stephanotis and statice), rinse the stems and spread them on newspapers to dry. No additional treatment is needed." She uses them as fillers in arrangements of fresh flowers from her yard or, even better, her neighbor's yard. Hughey also suggests, "To make cut flowers last longer, add two tablespoons of white vinegar and two tablespoons of sugar for each quart of water."

"Recycle Styrofoam packing peanuts and save money on potting soil by filling the bottom of your pot with several inches of peanuts, which provide excellent drainage for your plants." —*Emily Hatch*

Deborah Wyatt makes the most of a worn set of vinyl window blinds, cutting up the vinyl for garden markers, using the string to tie up plants, and using the top piece to stake plants.

Patricia Martin has a five-year-old basket of impatiens that she brings inside for the winter and then trims back each spring.

"Walk around your neighborhood and compliment your neighbors' and friends' yards, and they will gladly give you clippings or share bulbs." —*Lisa Kersey*

"For wildflowers for your home garden, visit a construction site and talk with a supervisor to see if you can dig up plants that are going to be bulldozed. He'll probably say 'help yourself' because they would otherwise be destroyed. You'll be surprised at what you will find." —*Bob Battle*

"I have a compost pile behind my house that provides me with rich compost that my neighbors and I can never get enough of; hence I try to make it as big as possible. When I see that someone in my neighborhood has bagged leaves and left them at the street for pickup by the city, I get my truck and load them up and take them to my compost pile. (a) I don't have to buy trash bags; (b) the leaves don't end up in the landfill; and (c) I get more compost to use in my garden." —*Jack Anderson*

> Without frugality, none can be rich and with it very few would be poor.
> —Samuel Johnson

"If you need a support for a vining plant growing near a column or wall, a length of string trimmer is ideal. It can be purchased in an almost clear color and becomes virtually invisible against a wall or other surface. It is very strong and can be cut to any length desired. It can also be used with wood or metal stakes to support plants that need to be staked. Its surface will not cut into plants when not on the string trimmer. It is very economical to use." —*Donna Davis*

Daisy Swarts had two spruce trees in pots on her patio that died. "Rather than buy new ones, I bought a cheap 99¢ can of outdoor spray paint in a natural-looking green shade and sprayed them. They have gone through a year and look great."

"My favorite household tip is to sprinkle Epsom salts on flowers and vegetable plants for healthier and longer lasting blooms." —Bruce Hawkins

"After your azaleas have quit blooming and all the buds have fallen off, water lightly for a couple of weeks and then start watering with two tablespoons of vinegar to one gallon of water. This will encourage more buds. This will work on most acid-loving plants." —Bruce Hawkins

"I save my vegetable and flower seed from each season to start my new garden." —Mary Bancroft

Bruce Hawkins has many uses for lady's hosiery, "From attractive legs to hanging out bulbs to dry." He also suggests, "After you wear them out good, cut them into strips for tying tomato plants and other plants."

"Use toilet paper rolls as individual planting pots. Place three seeds in each. When one has two pairs of leaves, strip off the other two to thin. This does not disturb the heartiest seedling. When the ground is warm enough, plant the entire tube with the plant." —Dixie Hopper

"To prevent your large container pots from becoming too heavy to move, fill them about halfway with old soda cans or plastic bottles. Then fill with soil and plant. This saves soil, improves drainage, and makes the pots lighter." —Bruce Hawkins

"Save your used tea bags and put them in a gallon jug of water and let set. When the time comes to water indoor plants, the brew is a great plant food, especially for ferns." —Kathy Jarrell

"When your handles break on your garden tools, don't toss them out. Stick the broken end in the ground and make a great trellis and conversation piece. You can let your vine grow up it with your shovel or rake end sticking out." —Bruce Hawkins

Tips: Saving in the Kitchen

"Buy plain bran and a box of raisins. This way the raisins will always be fresh. Put raisins in a glass container; if they seem dry, dampen a small piece of a paper towel to put with them. The raisins take up the moisture, and you always have fresh raisins." —Kathryn Groover

Shirley Birdwell says to wash and save the foam trays holding meats, cheese, and other grocery items: "They are perfect for travel and picnics."

Susan Hanks-Mowen recycles scallions. "I purchase the scallions with roots still remaining, even trimmed roots. I keep a pot of dirt going in the kitchen window, so after chopping the scallion almost all the way down, stopping about an inch above the root, I replant the scallion for a second go-round. It grows to almost full height and is just as delectable as the first time. Unfortunately, these roots are only good for two go-rounds."

"To remove a tight bottle cap, wrap a rubber band around the cap and twist." —*Robert Emans*

"Don't throw the zip bags away. After use, turn them inside out, wash them, and turn them over a jar or glass to dry." —*Nancy Lamb*

"I cut off the crust of my bread for some sandwiches. I freeze the crust and then use it for bread crumbs when I need some for a casserole." —*Esther Duckworth*

"I use the juice out of canned fruit for the second cup of liquid in Jell-O. It enhances the flavor." —*Marie Parish*

"Keep chopped onions and bell pepper in your freezer. You can save money on extra toppings when you order pizza. Just microwave the pepper and onion and add to pizza just before serving. If you are preparing frozen pizza, you can add these items plus chopped mushrooms, olive, cheese, or more pepperoni." —*Levern Kindred*

Terrie Dobbins buys two-liter bottles of cola and then pours them as needed into sixteen- and twenty-ounce bottles that she saves from previous uses. "Then I take the smaller one with me."

"Mix the crumbs in your cookie jar with brown sugar and a pinch of cinnamon. Add to your favorite coffee cake the next time you bake." —*Chyrie McKinney*

"Rather than running the water till it gets hot, wet the dishrag and place in the microwave for twenty-five seconds. To sterilize the dishrag, place in the microwave for thirty-five seconds." —*Bill Vaughn*

"To make milk stay fresh past the expiration date, add a pinch of salt. It will not change the taste." —*Eva Hollis*

"Vidalia onions are kept best if wrapped individually in old panty hose and hung to get plenty of fresh air." —*Bob Battle*

"When your Glade Plug-In refills dry up, cut them open and dump the dried-up liquid into your potpourri pot to boil. Also, when your candles burn down and there's some wax left that doesn't burn, dump them into the pot to boil. This tip is twofold: when you turn the pot off, sometimes it molds. Not so with the candle wax in there. It hardens and forms a seal—no more mold. Then when you turn it on again, the candle melts again and these really do add a nice smell to your home." —*Virginia Small*

"Three or four cakes can easily be iced with one can of ready-to-spread icing and done in a snap. Simply remove a third to a fourth of the icing and heat in the microwave until warm and slightly melted. Stir and drizzle over the cakes. Looks great for a third to half the cost and calories." —*Sharon Newman*

"When freezing bread, I always pull another bread bag over the loaf before freezing. I also use an entire half gallon of ice cream because I put it in a Tupperware container. It keeps without tasting like cardboard." —*Kathryn Groover*

"I use plastic bags and newspaper sleeves to pack my garbage in instead of buying garbage bags. I put a grocery paper bag in the garbage can." —*Kathryn Groover*

Betty Biles cuts her Brillo pads in half. "They last twice as long," she says.

Cathi Winkler's family of six likes "converted" or parboiled rice, such as Uncle Ben's, instead of plain white rice. But she "always hesitated buying it because of the cost, $4.79 for a five-pound bag. While shopping one day, I noticed that this same kind of rice was in the Mexican food section, under the brand name of Canilla Dorado. It was five pounds for $3.95. I have used it ever since," says Winkler.

"I have all of my meals (dinner) written down on three-by-five-inch cards. This helps me save time in planning meals and helps when I don't have time to make a grocery list. If I am on my way to the grocery store, I grab my cards for the week and I know exactly what to buy. I don't have to plan meals, I already have them written down, side dishes and all. This also keeps my husband from saying, 'we just had this last week.'" —*Sharon Kelley*

Donna Marcum chops fresh herbs into individual ice trays and covers them with water, freezes them, and stores them in zipper sandwich bags: "Drop the ice cubes in your cooking, and they taste fresh out of the garden—so much flavor and cheaper than the ones bought from the grocery."

Mary McEwen is a chicken expert, buying two ten-pound bags of legs at 19¢ a pound and cooking half of them to freeze in meal-size bags. The other half she boils, saving the meat for casseroles, salads, and croquettes. Then she saves the fat and broth for other uses.

"Our family loves the expensive, refrigerated, name-brand kosher dill pickles. After we finish a jar of these pickles, we save the pickle juice and spices that are in the bottom of the jar. We then purchase the cheaper store brand dill slices, drain off the pickle juice, and rinse them several times with cold water. The juices and spices from the expensive pickles are then added to these washed slices, shaken well, and refrigerated. After a couple of days, these dill slices taste completely different and are nearly as good as the very expensive pickles." —*Steve Maloney*

Beware of little expenses; a small leak will sink a great ship.
—Benjamin Franklin

"When you get to the bottom of a bag of potato chips and the chips get small and crumbly, transfer the chips to a zip bag and freeze for casserole toppings. Freeze Tostitos chips for Mexican dishes also." —*Ms. Bogle*

"A way to save money on dishwasher detergent is to put it only in one side of the washer dispenser. Put it in the wash cycle side on the right. Works beautifully for me." —*Sylvia Ogle*

"As soon as your meal is over, if you have leftover bread, crumble it, put it in a freezer bag, and place it in the freezer. Before you know it, you will have enough bread crumbs for your favorite recipe or dressing." —*Wilma Watson*

"Bake one can of biscuits (ten) and fry the same number of sausage patties. Cool and make ten sandwiches and freeze. They're very easy to heat in the microwave for a busy worker or for a school lunch." —*Belle Sturgill*

"Don't throw away those mesh bags that potatoes, oranges, or onions come in. Roll the bag into a ball or square and sew with heavy-duty thread, dental floss, or fishing line. It makes a great 'chore' pad for dishes, pots and pans, and even for dry skin. Try it." —*Inez Riley*

"Go meatless two or three times a week. At other meals, use meat as a side dish. This is better for your health and also costs less." —*Linda Rivers*

"I found that empty rice-boiling bags make wonderful gentle scrubbers for dishwashing. Just snip off the top, pour out the rice, and have months of free scrubber. I wash mine in the dishwasher from time to time, and it stays fresh and clean." —*Peg Kelly*

"I purchase packages of twelve to thirteen bath cloths to use as napkins. They can be thrown in and washed daily with other laundry and only need folding. Think how many paper napkins you save over a year's time" —*Wilma Cunningham*

"Make a cheap cookbook. I bought a photo album for $1 at a yard sale and am putting all of my recipes that I have collected from the newspaper in it." —*Mary Nell Paris*

"Need a wire whisk to incorporate eggs with milk, but too cheap to buy one? Use one of your mixer attachments!" —*Deborah Kay Lanius*

"Occasionally I have a dishcloth that needs brightening. I use a hard plastic bowl that also needs stains removed. I put a cap full of bleach into the water for that job. From there I use the liquid to clean a dirty ashtray. Then down the disposal. Voilà, four jobs for the price of one." —*Norma Doss*

"Rather than purchasing a ready-made can-stacking tier for your pantry, you can make one that fits your pantry shelf exactly. Cut two-by-four's the length of your shelf. Even one piece is a great help in raising a back row into view." —*Carol Ann Graham*

"Save the inner covers of your corn flakes and other cereal. This is a great weight of paper to put your cookie dough in to roll out before cutting with a cookie cutter." —*Margie Willis*

"Substitute a nutty breakfast cereal for expensive almonds in cake recipes. You will have delicious desserts with half the fat and calories." —*Pat Harper*

"To make heart-shaped cupcakes, don't buy a special pan. Just place a small marble or a half inch ball of aluminum foil between the cupcake liner and one side of the muffin tin." —*Dana Bates*

"You know the juice that can be strained off your canned veggies? Well, save it and freeze it. Then when you want to make homemade soup, it makes great soup stock." —*Beth McCracken*

"When very ripe bananas are on sale, buy a bunch. Peel, bag, and freeze them. Then when you make banana muffins or bread, remove as many as the recipe calls for, thaw, mash, and use as usual." —*Martha Jean Burris*

Avis June Thompson admitted that she washes and reuses her paper towels.

"A favorite use for newspaper sleeves is to fill them with onion peelings, cantaloupe peelings, and anything that smells and put the filled sleeve in my kitchen waste can. Then if it doesn't get emptied right away, I don't have to contend with smelly garbage." —*Virginia Small*

"I dump wet coffee grounds in newspaper bags, tie them, and toss. I also use the bags after a meal when I have table scraps to toss in the garbage. I clean paint brushes and store them in the bags." —*Neil Jordan*

Betty Biles rotates her dishes and glassware to equalize the wear and tear on them. "I realized that naturally the dishes and glassware I was using the most were going to wear a lot more than the dishes on the bottom and the glassware in the back of the cabinets. The dishes at the bottom should be rotated to the top of the stack, and the glasses in the front should be switched with the glasses in the back. That way dishes and glassware will not have to be replaced as often."

> My grandfather's motto is still the best advice I've heard: "One way to make money is not to spend it."
> —Michael Eisner, CEO of Disney

Bobbi Greene buys bone-in chicken breasts when she can find a "buy-one, get-one-free" deal, puts them all in a large stew pot with water and salt, and cooks them until they are very tender. Once they are cool, she removes the meat and discards all bones and skin. "This fabulous chicken is ready to be packaged in freezer bags and put in the freezer. Now you have a tremendous head start on terrific homemade meals like chicken divan, creamed chicken over corn bread, chicken salad, or chicken and noodles. This saves a lot of money and time."

Instead of pouring out "the water/ice/salt mixture after making home-made ice cream, pour it into half-gallon milk cartons and freeze. When ready to use, beat the cartons on all sides with a hammer to crush again. Pour mixture into the freezer bucket for reuse. You'll save the cost of ice and salt, plus a trip to the store." —*Josephine Roy*

Here are two clever uses for coffee filters: "If you are eating a popsicle, stick the stick through a coffee filter to keep it from dripping on you. If you are painting, put a coffee filter on the end of the paint brush to keep the paint from dripping on you." —*Ruby Miller*

Instead of buying the Swiffer or other similar products, Suzanne Adams just puts one of the Swiffer or Pledge wipes on her sponge mop and goes wherever she wants to dust.

Make your own personalized magnets. Michele Chaffin picks up advertising magnets at businesses whenever possible and personalizes them for friends (even Ms. Cheap) and relatives using some Elmer's glue and creativity. "In an effort to get my sister to quit smoking, I began with a most unattractive picture of her with a cigarette hanging out of her mouth. I then trimmed the photo to fit one of those advertising magnets. We now call them Frigee Photos."

Mary Lee Uster created the "ultimate (cheap and space-saving) salad spinner"—a white cotton pillowcase. She puts washed greens in the case and holds something under it as she runs outside. "I hold the case closed at the open end and twirl it around and around. The water comes out of the case and the lettuce, spinach, or greens are ready for your salad bowl. The only disadvantages to my spinner are the looks from your neighbors or guests while you are twirling."

"All salmon comes in olive-colored cans shaped like a drinking glass. The edges are smooth and won't cut you. Get the odor out with baking soda and vinegar. Make sure the inside dries so it won't rust. Makes handy patio or picnic glasses, and the color seems to be frosty." —*Evelyn Hooper*

"Save heavy wax paper from cereal boxes to freeze your meat in. Use the wax paper that soda crackers come in to bake Irish potatoes in the microwave." —*Kathryn Groover*

"Stop wasting money on potato chips. I found a way to bring stale chips back to life. Spread them out in a single layer on a baking sheet. Set them under the broiler for four minutes. It's like giving them CPR. You'll be saving money because your family will eat more from a larger bag." —*Joanne Waller*

Kathy Baldwin puts regular tea bags in the same box with flavored teas such as mint and orange. "The regular tea bags adopt their box-mates' flavor."

There's "no need to buy special cupcake pans. Put canning rings that you use to put on home-canning food upside down on a cookie sheet (about eighteen per cooking sheet). Use the same idea for freezing mini-salads. When frozen, put in plastic freezer bag." —*Ann Seiverling*

Vivian Anderson makes her own pancake syrup by adding a half cup of hot water to one cup of granulated sugar and bringing it to a boil. She adds either a little lemon juice or corn syrup (to keep them from sugaring) and a half teaspoon of maple flavoring, boiling a few minutes until "syrupy."

"I buy my butter or margarine in sticks rather than tubs. I keep the stick wrappers in a zip bag in the fridge. By wiping the pan surface with the buttery side of the wrapper, I not only save on spray but save waste that would otherwise have gone in the trash with the wrapper. Now that's cheap, but it works." —*Joe Cormier*

"I save all of the medicine cups from the hospital and ask some of my friends to save them for me if I run short. I make pesto in the summer when my herb garden is in, fill the little one-and-a-half-ounce cups, set them on a plate, and freeze them. I then put them back in a zip bag and into the freezer. One little cup makes a wonderful lunch with a bowl of spaghetti. I do the same with the unused portion of tomato sauce or paste from a recipe. This idea is wonderful for a cook who lives alone." —*Florence Conner*

"I'm the only one in my house who drinks coffee; I just drink one to two cups per day, and I hate having to make it every morning. So I make a pot on Monday morning and let it cool and put it in a Tupperware container and refrigerate it. Then whenever I desire, I pour a cup, put it in the microwave on the coffee setting, and I have a fresh cup of coffee. This saves me time, energy, and money." —*Beth McCracken*

"Make your own egg substitute to save the high cost of the commercial product. Buy eggs when they are on sale and separate the yolk from the white. Combine one yolk with a dozen egg whites for flavor and color and freeze in ice cube trays until needed." —*Jackie Brown*

"The salad bar at your favorite grocery can be a source of significant savings as it was for me recently. I was making a recipe that called for some chopped celery. I don't eat celery, so I didn't want to buy a bunch. Instead I bought what I needed from the salad bar. This also works great for things like mushrooms and cheese." —*John Henderson*

"To flavor my coffee each morning, I use the milk left on my kids' cereal. I save on milk and sweetener." —*Kris Powell*

"Recycle coffee grounds. If you need to make a second pot in the morning or anytime, use the grounds from the first pot plus add one half that amount to the next pot. It does better than you might think." —*June Thompson*

 Barbara Stewart says the fastest and best way to dry herbs is to spread them out in one layer on microwave paper towels and microwave them for two minutes at full power. Continue in thirty-second intervals if necessary and cool for about ten minutes. Store in opaque air-tight containers and freeze up to six months. This leaves the herbs with more of their original color and flavor than air drying does."

Corrine Fuson has this idea for a bag holder for her accumulating grocery bags: "Take a gallon milk jug, turn it upside down, and cut off the bottom. That will be the top. Cut a little bit around the pouring spout too. That will be where you pull the bags through. Take a staple gun and attach it to a wall. Bags can be put in and pulled out through the bottom."

"Instead of throwing away broth off chicken, I freeze it and use it to flavor ramen noodles or other dishes." —*Wilma Pearl Slayton*

"After using a soapy steel wool pad, put it in the freezer—it will thaw quickly for its next use and won't be rusty." —*Pat Helm*

"Buy tuna—it's the cheapest protein."
—*Joyce Wing*

"Don't buy liquid hand soap for the kitchen or bathroom. Just buy antibacterial dish liquid and put part of this cleaner in pump bottles. You can even dilute it with a little water." —*Susan Goebel*

"I always wash off my aluminum foil and zip bags. I put my glass in the freezer so I keep the same glass all day (I rinse after each use)." —*Consondra Loughran*

"I make two pots of coffee in the A.M.—one for the thermos and one we drink. I use the same filter. Saves a filter and the coffee tastes great." —*Marjo Allen*

"Instead of ground beef in my favorite spaghetti sauce, I cut up yellow squash, zucchini, onion, and mushrooms into chunks and sauté al dente. It's healthier and cheaper." —*Martha Plunkett*

"Put hose with runs in them in the kitchen. Cut them to the size of a rolling pin, wet the rolling pin, and put the hose on the rolling pin. The dough will not stick." —*Lynn Yuchnitz*

"Dry and then reuse tea bags." —*Joyce Wing*

"To make a very handy cooking oil bottle to use at the stove, use an ordinary water bottle with the pull-up sport top. Just fill it with oil. It is so much easier than trying to pour from a large jug into a skillet." —*Corrine Fuson*

"To make my sloppy joes go farther, I drain and wash a can of kidney beans and add them to the mixture. They add protein and complex carbohydrates without the fat. You can also chop or mash them before you add them to disguise the mixture." —*Lynn Batey*

"When making chicken stock for soup or other dishes, make four extra cups. Strain and chill to separate the chicken fat. Skim most of the fat off and pour the room-temperature broth into ice cube trays to freeze. Pop out as many cubes as desired to make gravy, to flavor the cooking water for rice and vegetables, or to serve as starter for chicken soup." —*Terry Schenk*

"Save your banana peels—blend with a small amount of water and put around your rose plants. Your roses will love you." —*Bruce Hawkins*

"When I buy hamburger or hot dog rolls at the bread thrift store, I select the large packages—the size that restaurants use—twenty-four to thirty-six rolls per package. I bag the amount my family can use and give the remainder to friends at work who have large families and are in need. Be sure to rebag rolls in plastic zip bags, and they will keep a long time." —*Joyce Hughey*

Corrine Fuson uses clear shower caps for large bowl covers. "You get a package of fifteen at Dollar General for $1, and they are big enough to cover huge bowls, even a thirteen-by-nine-inch pan. Since they are clear, you can see what is inside, and they are inexpensive enough to throw away. Once you try these, you will never go back to plastic wrap."

Terry Schenk says the quickest and easiest way to get all of the tomato paste or pumpkin pie puree out of a can is to cut off both the top and bottom of the can. "Remove the bottom lid carefully and have a container ready. Push on the top lid and the paste will slide out cleanly into the bowl. Carefully remove the top lid and wipe off any paste clinging to it."

Tips: Laundry

"To save laundry detergent, hot water, and about fifteen minutes, stop the washer at the end of the wash cycle for a load of white clothes. Remove clothes to a dish pan or bucket, draining soapy water back to the washer. Put in a load of colored clothes, reset washer to wash, and let it run through the entire cycle. Then put the whites back in and set the washer at spin and rinse and finish the load." —*Janet Keim*

"Once a year, I run my washer through the cycle with a gallon of vinegar. It saves on plumbing bills—the vinegar takes all the sludge out of the pipes." —*Betty Horton*

"I wash my clothes by hand in gallon buckets right after I wear them. I save the water and use it as a toilet flusher, remembering to leave plenty of water in the bowl. The force of pouring the water from the bucket keeps the sewage line unstopped, clean, and clear." —*Mitchell Plowden*

"Save ten minutes of dryer time by washing at night and leaving the washer lid open overnight. When you use your dryer in the morning, you will save approximately ten minutes of dryer time." —*Betty Horton*

"Hand-washable clothes do well in Suave shampoo instead of the name-brand delicate detergents." —*Mary Carter*

"If you have empty rooms upstairs, run two clotheslines. Since heat goes up, you have a cheap way to dry clothes in the winter months without using your dryer." —*Sammy Angel*

"Tear your dryer sheets in half and double your amount per box." —*Angela Freund*

"Use a half cup of white vinegar instead of fabric softener," says Leona Harris. She noted that it is cheaper, and the clothing smells fresh and is clean and soft.

6

Saving on Family and Fun

The whole point of being cheap is to get the most for your money. That way, whatever you save can be used for something else. This is particularly true with families and fun because there is just as much free and fun stuff to do as there is expensive stuff. So if you take advantage of the freebies most of the time, you may still have enough resources to occasionally indulge in something a little pricier. I still don't think many of us can "do it all," but this way, we can do a lot more!

This chapter also includes some award-winning tips from young people who are starting early with frugality and smart spending.

Tips: Saving with Children

"Save the colored caps from spray cans, wash thoroughly, and check rims for sharp edges. We have no children in our home, but these make great toys for visiting children. They can be used again and again after thorough washing." —*Levern Kindred*

Alan Dooley built his children a tree house for $250 instead of the $700 to $800 it would have cost without his ingenuity. He used windows and doors, concrete blocks, and steps from a reuse center, scrap from a roofing company for the roof, stain mixed together from "Oops" paints at Home Depot, and wood scraps from a residential building site. "It is a big hit with my son and daughter and their friends. With the toys that we were able to move out to the playhouse, I was able to empty out the children's side of the playroom. The former half-playroom/half-office is now all my home office, saving office rent and allowing a full deduction for the room as a home office."

"A standard pillowcase slips over a bassinet mattress to make an ideal two-sided cover for a new baby. A king-sized pillowcase fits a cradle mattress to make a two-sided cover for baby's bed." —*Mary Suliano*

"I save five-pound netted potato sacks for tub toys. When the children are done playing with them, I put them in the bag and hang it on the shower organizer; all of the excess water drains into the tub. No mildew on the toys." —*Tammy Steele*

"Plan Halloween costumes so they can double as pajamas for the kids later . . . a pink sleeper with feet was part of a pig costume." —*Nina Nissen*

Avis June Thompson made a special book for her one-year-old grand-daughter—featuring photographs of family members.

Tracey Campbell sent this recipe for homemade baby wipes: "I've used these for about two years now. The store-bought containers of wipes aver-age $2 or more each, and with two babies in diapers at one time, we used one per week, spending $8 a month. The approximate cost of the homemade wipes is 50¢ per box. By using them, we spend for a whole month what we previously spent for one container. Here's how: Buy a roll of Bounty paper towels. (You really can't skimp and buy a cheaper brand as they won't hold up.) Cut the roll in half and remove the cardboard tube. Into an old pop-up wipe container, pour approximately one-half cup warm water. Placing the cut side down, put one of the paper towel halves inside. Mix together an additional one to two cups water and a few drops each of baby oil and liquid and pour over the paper towels. Be sure of course to keep these tightly covered or they will dry out."

> Money is like sex. If your children don't learn about it from you, they'll learn about it from their friends.
>
> —Knight Ridder News Service

"Sign up the kids for the birthday club at places like Shoney's and Captain D's, and they will send a coupon for a free meal or dessert on their birthday." —*Eric Heikkenen*

"Take the kids to live remote broadcasts on Saturdays at car dealers if free refreshments (hot dogs, sodas, etc.) are being served." —*Nina Nissen*

"When a child is born in your family, save the whole paper to give him or her in later years. It really doesn't take much room in a cedar chest and is a neat gift." —*Linda Dixon*

"Make a backyard sprayer for your children. Cut a few slits on one side of a two-liter soda bottle. Insert the garden hose and tape well with electrical tape. Turn on the water, and they will be pleasantly surprised." —*June Thompson*

"To supplement my girls' play kitchenware, I save the plastic containers from items such as Hershey's cocoa, Nesquick powdered drink mix, and candy sprinkles. These make good play kitchen items and last longer than the ones you can purchase at a toy store." —*Jeannie Halenda*

"Save thousands of dollars over a two-and-a-half-to-three-year period by washing cloth diapers instead of buying expensive landfill-clogging disposables. Advertisers would have us believe that cloth diapers are less sanitary and more trouble. This isn't so. I have never used disposables on my two children. Cloth diapers are simply laundry." —*Mary Carter*

Kathy Buker made a playhouse for her two-year-old from a dishwasher carton. "I peaked the roof with the flaps at the top. I cut the door by just cutting it on three sides and folding it out. I then decorated it with different wallpapers, one color for roof, one for walls. I cut strips of fabric and hot-glued them on the inside next to the windows. This toy was used for four years by both my children, and it cost me nothing."

Corine Sandifer found a creative reuse for empty roll-on deodorant containers: "Take off the top roller and fill with poster paints. Replace the top and let your child paint. This also cuts down on the mess and storing of poster paints." She also suggests cutting up a credit card to make several guitar picks and an ice scraper.

Dana Bates said that when her children complete their artwork on their at-home easels, she saves it and uses it as wrapping paper for grandparents' gifts.

The mother of four very sports-minded (and constantly thirsty) children, Stacy Ross earned the title of the "Cheap Gatorade Queen" by mixing her own instead of buying the expensive prepared bottles. "Would you believe that I pay 29¢ per quart for the same drink by mixing my own? The bottles recycle wash after wash. We figure that we save nearly $200 a year in mixing our own Gatorade," she boasts. "The greatest advantage besides the cost is the convenience of always having it on hand."

"At a little girl's birthday party, use real teacups and saucers purchased at thrift stores. We outfitted a party for ten for less than $5 and then sent the cups and saucers home as favors. The girls were very pleased to use 'real china,' and we saved money on the paper products. The table looked great, and we had no extra expense for favors." —*Jennifer Ardis*

"Do not throw away used plastic ware. Wash and reuse or let the kids use it for paint, sand, etc." —*Sherry Cox*

"Instead of buying school pictures through the school, I try to take the kids to a picture studio before Christmas. The school pictures rarely come out well, and I can get three times as many pictures for the same price from a studio like the ones in Wal-Mart or Kmart. These studios also take their time taking the pictures, and they come out better. They make great Christmas gifts." —Diane Ballard

"Living in a two-story home with children, I always worry about escaping a fire. Commercial fire ladders are too big and bulky and heavy for children to handle themselves, not to mention costly. I have gathered lots of old sheets from garage sales at $1 to $3 a set and tied them together with big knots spaced a foot apart. I've anchored them to bed frames and stored them under each bed. In case of an emergency, the kids can easily throw it out the window and climb down to safety." —Kris Powell

"My little granddaughter, Alexa, and I frequently use an Easy Bake Oven to make cakes and other goodies. Instead of buying their mixes, which cost $2.40 for a one-layer iced cake, I use regular cake mixes and canned icing, which costs a lot less. I use mixes that just need water added and store the unused part in the refrigerator. The unused icing is also stored in the refrigerator. Alexa just takes a spoonful out of the can, and we soften it in the microwave." —June Ross

"We take our own thirty-five millimeter pictures of Santa with the kids at the mall, develop them promptly, and frame them for Christmas. We save $8 a picture." —Jill Baker

"We use our son's bathwater to water plants, indoor and outdoor. We just get a bucket, scoop out the water, and water the plants. They don't know the difference." —*Clay Dyer*

"Instead of buying a bassinet in preparation for my last child, I went to a toy store and bought a large heavy-duty plastic wagon. I had measured beforehand and found that a porta-crib mattress fit well into the bed of the wagon. This became my bassinet and was very handy for transporting the baby around the house. After the baby grew out of the bassinet stage, I took the mattress out and now have a wagon for the boys to play in and for gardening purposes. My husband couldn't decide if this was one of my crazier ideas or one of my smartest." —*Karen Gillette*

There must be more to life than having everything.
—Maurice Sendak

Gayle Anderson says after her children play in the plastic wading pool in the summer, she organizes a "bucket brigade" where they can fill as many buckets as the pool holds and empty them onto plants in the garden. "The kids love doing this, and the plants benefit as well. We also save water by using it twice."

Kimberly Borum makes her own frozen slush drinks for her children using frozen strawberries. She not only saves money, but makes something healthy, too. "I got out my blender and some frozen presweetened strawberries that I thawed slightly in the microwave, added crushed ice and some water (two parts ice, one part water), gave it a whirl in the blender, and told my kids it was a strawberry Icee. My oldest daughter proclaimed my new Icee invention was better than the store-bought kind."

Lisa Kersey teamed with her hubby to make a puppet-show theater for their three young daughters. They patterned their theater after one Lisa had seen in a catalog for $225 and ended up making it for $15—the cost of a sheet of plywood, which they combined with some leftover two-by-fours and leftover paint. Lisa made curtains out of material a friend gave her and ended up with the best gift of the year. "My husband and I had lots of fun making something together, and the girls just expect one gift from us now instead of many."

> Nothing is cheap which is superfluous, for what one does not need is dear at a penny.
> —Plutarch

Mary Chapman occasionally entertains her children and their friends with undecorating the house, unloading unwanted items, and doing ungames like the fastest at untying a shoe or the fastest at going under a table. "They wear their shirts backwards and change their names, and in the games we mix up turns because everyone is so unorganized."

Mary Shelton said she volunteers to drive on school field trips: "You can see great plays (generally much better than adult theater) for free, plus the before-show entertainment is great."

When her baby was eight months old, Gwen Dyer called the different baby product companies and requested coupons. "I have saved oodles of money. They all sent coupons for a variety of products."

"Freeze water in milk jugs or any large container. Then remove the container and give the kids the huge block of ice. They can do so many creative things with them. Have a contest to see who can sit on the block of ice the longest. Melt hot pennies into them, make an ice sculpture, or just lick it until it melts." —*Corine Sandifer*

"When knee holes in pants are beyond repair, cut them off into shorts. Also cut off babies' 'onesies' to make great shirts. When they are too short to snap, they usually fit everywhere else . . . for another year or so." —*Mary Carter*

A good way to teach children the value of saving is to have a piggy bank in the kitchen set aside for a goal. She and her son saved up for a VCR years ago by putting change in a jar. "It made quite an impression on him of how a little can add up to a lot." —*Mary Claire Bradshaw*

Do you have a small child who begs for his own room? I did and solved the problem by putting him in a closet. We took the (sliding) doors off, built in a bed, put shelves on three sides, put a lift-up door under the bed for toy storage and, presto, a place of his own. The room was at the end of a hall, which made it nice and private." —*Linda Dixon*

"When your children outgrow their pajamas with feet, cut off the feet for extended wear (the pajamas of course)." —*Janice Derrickson*

Barb Augustine says for a child's birthday party, she reuses the invitation as a gift tag/birthday card to put on the gift her child takes to the party. "I just write on the back of it."

Barbara Reed organizes neighborhood summer play groups as an alternative to day camp. "Start with eight to ten children of the same age. Our play group met once a week from 9:00 A.M. to 1:00 P.M. Each mom took a turn planning and hosting the play groups. We had a theme for each play date, and games, art activities, outdoor water play, and pizza lunches."

"One of the best cheap lunches my daughter loves is a scoop of peanut butter in a reusable container and some pretzels. She loves to dip the pretzels in the peanut butter. In our house, we don't buy Lunchables. This is our alternative and we call it our 'cheapables.'" —*Corinne Sandifer*

"Huggies Little Swimmers swim diapers can be used many times; simply dry after each use, except, of course, when they get soiled." —*Kathy Harwell*

"When you see cute kids' clothes on sale, but they are too large, go ahead and buy them. Kids grow!" —*Nancy Green*

☺ "When your kids want juice, fill the cup half full of water and half full of their favorite juice. It will save you money, and you are getting them to drink water." —*Lakisha Randolph*

The Next Generation of Cheapos!

We had a contest in *The Tennessean* in which we invited cheapos under eighteen years old to send in their best money-saving tips. Look what they sent in:

"If you need stationery but don't have the money, use the Sunday comics and glue the characters on paper and envelopes. It's very pretty and cheap. You can use Nancy, Peanuts, Beetle Bailey, Marvin, and Baby Blues." —*Anna Avery, ten*

"My friend and I take turns driving each other to and from school. One week I take her, and the next week, we reverse and she takes me. This gives me extra cash to do things with my friends on weekends that I otherwise wouldn't have been able to cover." —*Melissa Thompson, sixteen*

"Use plastic bags from the grocery store or department store or newspaper bags to make hair ties. Cut into one-to-two-inch strips, the length of the bag; use three strips and braid the plastic. Tape the end to a table or clipboard, and then cut off the ends. This can be tied like a ponytail holder or under the back of your hair as a headband." —*Carrie Bryant, ten* (Carrie also braided plastic bags to make a jump rope and made a denim scarf out of a pair of jeans she had cut off to make shorts.)

Abbie Ardis shared these tips when she was ten years old: "Enter any and all contests and drawings. I have won a bike, two birthday parties, pizzas, dolls, a chair, circus tickets, shoes, and money. Sometimes you just enter your name, sometimes color a picture, or even run a race. In the race, I was the only one to enter in my age group and I won the Nikes."

Abbie Ardis was nine years old when she submitted these "kids' cheap ideas": "Let your mom shop for you at thrift stores. A hermit crab is a great pet: they cost only $4, a jar of food lasts forever, and there are no vet bills. Be sure to put your lost teeth under your pillow for the tooth fairy.Don't pay over $8 for a Beanie Baby. Sell your old toys at consignment stores."

"Instead of buying your dog expensive chew toys, give him empty plastic Coke or Gatorade bottles. We take the caps off because the dog will chew them off. You can also buy rope at Home Depot and tie knots in it instead of buying the expensive rope chew toys they sell for dogs." —*Alexandra Seamens, ten*

Lacy Broemel, nine, is big into cardboard, making doll house furniture and other items, like a garden and a doll bowling alley, out of a box. She also made a garage for toy cars.

Twins Jason and Jeremy Gregory, ten, and their sister Jessica, six, are all on the cheap path. Jason uses the back of used paper from his dad's printer for drawing pictures, crafts, and scrap paper. He rents video games and checks out books from the library before buying them to be sure he likes them. Jeremy helps his dad in the yard by using grass clippings around bushes and trees instead of mulch. He says he also uses the gift certificates he gets during the year at after-Christmas sales. Jessica likes to grow flowers from seeds: "This is cheaper and I can watch them grow from the beginning."

"My mom and I use brown paper bags to wrap gifts and use rubber stamps to decorate the bags. This is fun and saves money on wrapping paper." —*Trey Woodard, eight*

"I love to spend and save money at the same time. Whenever I go to the mall, I hardly even look at the regular-priced clothes, but instead I make a beeline to the clearance racks. I also go to outlet malls and search for clothes that have problems." —*Hilary Few, fourteen*

Jennifer Yuchnitz, thirteen, says that if eyeglasses can't be repaired, she saves all the screws (usually six per pair) to use on other glasses.

She also saves the nose pieces to reuse. Her family donates old glasses to eye stores, which send them to poor countries.

Taylor Bates, five, duct-tapes toilet paper rolls together to make a tunnel that he uses to talk to his little brother. He also cuts out coupons, paints gourds, and uses his cleaned-up sandbox toys to make cool-shaped Jell-O.

"My mom opened a savings account for me. Whenever I make a deposit, my mom and grandmother match the amount so I can triple my deposit with their help each time. My mom will not let me take any out once it goes in, and she goes over my bank statement with me so I can see how the amount gets bigger." —*Garrett Neimer, eight*

Rebecca Barden, eleven, learned the hard way after seeing a fake nail kit on TV. She saved up her allowance and bought the $20 kit. It looked so pretty: a few different colors of nails and a gadget that held all the decorative stuff, glitter, and decals. But when she used it, the gadget fell apart, the nails fell off, and she got really annoyed. She says, "Now I always go check out the thing I want to buy, and if I keep thinking about it for a few weeks, I will buy it. Now everything I buy is worth it."

Tips: Saving with Pets

"For a cheap, functional, sturdy, and washable kitty litter box, use a covered plastic storage box with a sealing lid. You can remove the lid for cleaning, scooping, and refilling. Cut a door in one end for the cat to enter." — *Deborah Reynolds*

"Dog biscuits can get expensive. We either break them in half or give the dogs something else. In the summer, for example, we give them a piece of 'candy'—an ice cube—as a treat. Now that is really cheap!" —*Sarah Dotson*

"Instead of buying those expensive dog treats, save money by making your own. Combine 2 cups flour, 1¼ cup shredded cheese, 2 cloves minced garlic, and ½ cup vegetable oil. Roll out and cut into shapes. A drinking glass works for round ones. Bake at 400 degrees for 10 to 15 minutes." —*Vicki White*

"I needed a bed for my Great Dane but almost had a heart attack at the price. So instead, I bought a twin bed foam pad and folded it in three. I then bought a twin sheet that matched our bed linen (his bed is in our bedroom) and sewed three sides and Velcro'd the fourth. That way I can throw the cover in the wash." —*Tina Cozby*

Wayne King found a cheap way to keep his distance from unleashed dogs while bicycling: a couple of squirts with a water pistol filled with ammonia and water. "They stopped in their tracks, turned tail, and went home. The smell of the ammonia seemed to deflate their egos instantly." For the cost of "one squirt gun and about 25¢ worth of ammonia and water, I have acquired a defensive instrument with about one hundred shots that reach ten to fifteen feet (compared to about six feet for expensive Mace), and I don't even have to be a good shot."

"Use duct tape to clean pet hairs from car upholstery." —*Frances McGill*

"I buy stuffed animals (at Goodwill) to use for toys for my dogs. They chew on them and not the expensive ones from the pet stores." —*Jackie Szadkowski*

"Why waste money on those pricey dog beds? Use shredded paper from the office or home to stuff a used pillowcase. Fasten it with a bread twist tie and you have a free bed. Place in a box or basket (purchased at Goodwill). When soiled, simply trash the paper, wash the pillowcase, and start over. Use a standard size for a small pet and king for a larger pet. To splurge, add a few cedar chips." —*Joyce Hughey*

Tips: Entertaining and Being Entertained

"After you use birthday candles, save them. When you remove them from the cake, place them in a cup of water. After the party is over, wash them in warm soapy water and allow them to dry completely. Put them in a zip bag until they are needed for the next birthday cake." —*Darlene Gentry*

"When I get invited to a Tupperware, Home Interior, or candle party, instead of buying something, I volunteer to have a party. As I start to call my friends for the invite, I have a list of snacks I am going to serve. If they ask, 'Can I bring something?' I say, 'Sure, could you bring a two-liter Coke?' and then mark it off the menu. Besides, the host always gets a free gift for having the party. If you don't need it, save it and use it for a wedding gift." —*Carolyn Marlin*

"A great way to attend events and visit great places for free is to volunteer. You can see and do some pretty cool things just by volunteering a little of your time." —*Mike McAlister*

"I suggest giving two dinner parties or cookouts on two successive days or nights. As long as you are going to the trouble and expense, this is the best way to go. The two parties will cost only about one and a half of what two would cost given separately because of the money you save on odds and ends. Also the energy of cleaning and setting up is expended only once." —*Joyce Henderson*

Velma Thompson and her neighbor take turns renting movies each weekend. "At Movie Gallery we can rent new releases for two nights for $3.98 and older releases for the same amount of time for $2.99. Since we rent movies frequently, this has turned out to be a great money saver for both of our families."

"Don't get cable. Just read the TV schedule and ask friends to tape shows that you really want to see. You can buy cheap tapes and use them over and over." —*the "Cheap Creep"*

"For family outings like picnics, give everyone a large sturdy plastic cup. Ask them to write their name on it and keep it for refills. You can even give them a plastic bag to keep the cup in. This decreases the need to use new paper cups every few minutes, not to mention the amount of litter to gather up. It will amaze you." —*Mary McEwen*

Tips: Saving on Reading

"A friend and I share a magazine subscription." —*Pam Barber*

Wayne King stretches his magazine subscriptions by suspending half of his subscriptions for six months at a time while he catches up on reading back issues. "Then after six months, I start getting the suspended ones and suspend the other half of the ones I had been getting. Sure enough, I don't have the piles of back reading that I used to and I am doubling my subscription money's worth."

"Read twelve for the price of one. Each member of a group of twelve (bridge club, church, office, exercise group) buys a great book on sale in

January, reads it, and swaps it off alphabetically when the group con-
venes each month, until all books have been read by all members. Each
member has enjoyed twelve good reads and has one great book to place
on a shelf or under a lamp." —*Betty C. Jones*

"To save on magazines, form a group of people who like to read them
but hate the cost. Each person orders one magazine, so there are no dupli-
cates. Once it's read, pass it along to the group. Put your name on it after
you've read it so others will know to whom to pass it." —*Cheryl Stewart*

"I persuaded three tenants in my apartment building to share the daily
paper. Two of us are early risers, so we read the paper first and pass it on
to the late sleeper, who then puts it outside the door of the fourth person, who likes to read at night." —*Mary McEwen*

"Instead of buying Ms. Cheap's book, I read a friend's copy." —*Linda
Culbreath*

 Lynn Yuchnitz suggests, "When you subscribe to a magazine,
write on the calendar the month the subscription will expire.
Renewals usually come through the mail a couple of months early." By
knowing when to renew, you can hold onto your money rather than
sending it to the magazine company earlier than necessary.

 "Don't buy a newspaper—go to the library to read it." —*Kerry
Sells*

☼ Tips: Restaurants

"When eating out at a restaurant, always order water instead of paying for a beverage. It saves money for a dessert." —*Nancy Ledford*

"When dining out, have one or more quart-size zip bags in your purse to bring home uneaten food to eat later or feed the pets or birds." —*Margarette Brown*

"I bring a can of soda into a restaurant and order a cup of ice. I pull the can out of my pocket or my wife's purse (she gets really embarrassed), and I've saved over a dollar." —*Clay Dyer*

"McDonald's has cheap hamburgers on Wednesdays. We take our own cheese, lettuce, tomato, and onion to put on top. We get two large fries and two large drinks, and for $7 our family of four eats very well." —*Sam and Debbi Scott*

Margaret Rolfe found a clever way to get a Caesar salad with fried chicken for $1.98, plus tax: "Go through the Wendy's drive-in window, purchase a Caesar side salad for 99¢, then purchase four chicken nuggets for 99¢. Cut up the nuggets and add to the Caesar salad. Enjoy!" The prices may change, but the strategy should be timeless.

"Order an entree that includes the soup and salad bar. Ask for a container to take the entree home with you for your next meal. Then go to the salad bar and pig out. This is not just cheap. It's smart." —*Marie Jett*

"When you eat at a fast food restaurant, always order the small drink if they have a self-serve fountain." —*Mary Ann Liden*

"Eat at home whenever possible! Learn to cook. Going out will be a special event instead of an expensive routine." —*Mary Carter*

Annette Whitefield is counting on her eyes being bigger than her stomach: "As a family, we go to Ponderosa when they offer a particular meal on special with the buffet at nearly the same price as the buffet. We order the special to go and fill up on the buffet. Then we put the special in the refrigerator, and that is the next evening's meal."

"For clean hands when dining out, save the wads of cotton stuffed in medicine bottles. Put them in a small jar. Pour some alcohol on the cotton and close the lid tight. Keep in your purse or car and, when ready to eat, take out a wad of cotton and clean hands. It's much cheaper than wet wipes." —*Mary McEwen*

"When husband and wife eat out, each order different dishes that they both would like to try and then, when the food arrives, share it." —*Isabelle Turner*

"Whenever possible, I order meals from the children's section of the menu. I am an average-sized woman, and those portions are enough. Not only do I save money, but I save on calories too." —*Kaysie Poulsen*

Tips: Holidays

"Instead of using store-bought ornaments, we adorn our Christmas tree with two cheap but meaningful kinds of ornaments: (1) ticket stubs from special artistic, cultural, and sporting events we attended and (2) inexpensive metallic or Plexiglas souvenir key chains we purchase on family trips (far cheaper than 'official' holiday ornaments). When we decorate for the holidays, we are reminded of good times together, and of course, we have stayed cheap!" —*Jim, Sue, Carolyn, Tom, and Allison Pichert*

"Find a 2-to-2½-foot branch with several small branches on it. Spray it white to use for decorations at different times of the year. For Valentine's Day, take the red envelopes you saved from Christmas and cut various-sized valentines from them. Cut shamrock leaves from the green envelopes for St. Patrick's Day. Redress the branch again with plastic Easter eggs." —*Margarette Brown*

Instead of buying the expensive cardboard containers to store wrapping paper and ribbons, make your own by using a traveling bag for suits or dresses. "Place rolls of paper upright in the part for suits and dresses and use the zip pockets to hold ribbon, gift cards, etc. Hang in the closet; you always know where the paper is, and it does not take up much space." —*Charlene Dew*

"Whenever someone in our immediate family receives a gift in a gift bag, of course we reuse the gift bags. But I have also found a way to

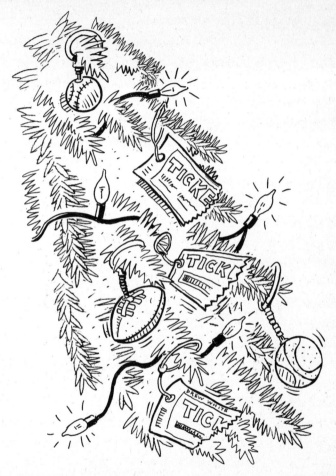

Instead of using store-bought ornaments, we adorn our Christmas
tree with two cheap but meaningful kinds of ornaments:
ticket stubs and souvenir key chains.

reuse the crumpled and already wrinkled tissue paper. Simply take a warm (not hot) iron and press the paper flat again. When the paper cools, it is flat, smooth, and crisp again, just like new." —*Stacy Dunaway*

"I often make little bags of goodies with holiday candy, and this year I realized that I can buy Christmas candy cheap after Christmas, separate the colors, and use them for the next two holidays. The red ones are great for Valentine's Day and the green ones for St. Patrick's Day; the gold and silver go for either. A Hershey Kiss that is a month old is still great." —*Sharon*

"You can make seasonal place mats by simply saving old Christmas, Easter, birthday, and other cards. Cut out the decorative part of cards in any shape and glue them together to make a place mat. The final step is to cover the place mat with clear contact paper. It is a great project for kids and an inexpensive way to decorate your table for the holidays and celebrations." —*Suzanne Albright*

"I reuse the same Easter baskets each year until they become too worn, filling them with stuff of my own choosing." —*Consondra Loughran*

"Buy new Christmas cups at the Goodwill stores and fill them with candy or flowers to give at Christmastime. The cups are plentiful after the Christmas season and can be bought cheaply and saved for next year. They are great for teachers and people in nursing homes or senior centers, and so on." —*Shirley Robertson*

7

Travel for Less

Don't Forget Frugality When Traveling

I was intrigued by an article from Debt Counselors of America on "How to Come Back from Vacation with Money in Your Pocket." How could that be? We've been on a lot of vacations, and I don't remember coming back with much money left over. Ever. It's so easy to get into that vacation mentality of spending, especially with fixed costs like hotels, food, attractions, and souvenirs. But fortunately, there are ways to keep vacation costs down without cutting down on the fun:

- Plan ahead, starting with a realistic budget of what you can afford for the vacation. Begin saving for your vacation in plenty of time to have enough money to make the trip. Have a yard sale or other family project to raise trip money. Designate your coupon savings or a portion of your paycheck each pay period for the trip. If your children are old enough, get them involved in the clipping.

- Be flexible about when you go and where you go. If your children are not school age or if you don't have children, go off-season and save big bucks. As far as a destination, let the deals guide you, instead of the other way around.

- Visit relatives. You can stay in their house, they can be your tour guides, and they might even cook a few meals for you.

- Vacation with another family or friends. You can split the cost of the condominium or house and share cooking, baby-sitting, and the like. We have done this at the beach since our children were little, and not only is it cheaper, but it's better, especially since our friends are magnificent cooks and lots of fun.

- Consider heading out for a trip to a state park. Rates are almost always reasonable, and there is a lot to do, with lakes, tennis, swimming, hiking, biking, and horseback riding. Almost every state has a great program, particularly for a family vacation. Many parks have cabins, and of course, camping is even cheaper.

- Check out travel books from the library instead of buying them.

- Get coupons and information off the Internet.

- If you're going to a city that has an *Entertainment Book,* consider buying one. These coupon books usually cost $20 to $25 but can save bundles on meals, attractions, car rentals, and airline tickets. (To order, call 1-800-374-4464.)

- It's obviously cheaper to drive than to fly. And when you drive, you can take things with you like spices, condiments, and a cooler (which you should take on any trip, loaded with drinks and snacks to avoid the interstate prices).

- If you're flying, Debt Counselors of America says call three airlines or use a travel agent to compare prices. And start early. "You may be able to get a cheap fare through a consolidator or discount travel agency. Pay with your credit card, if possible, and be sure you understand all restrictions and refund policies."

- Get a kitchen or kitchenette so you can cook at least a couple of meals a day. Eating out is fun, but the cost sure can add up.

- Check out colleges and universities to see if they rent out dormitory rooms during nonschool times. (Bill Hughey suggests consulting the *Norman J. Peterson Directory* at the library and then calling toll-free numbers.) Not only can you get a cheap room, but sometimes you get access to their facilities, like laundry, pool, fitness, or tennis.

- Consider staying in a hotel or motel on the outskirts of the city you want to visit. These places are usually cheaper.

- Find a hotel with a complimentary breakfast. This can be big savings for a family of four. Not only do you get a good breakfast, but you can take an apple or banana for a later snack.

- It is often cheaper and better to make the hotel reservation directly with the hotel instead of calling the chain's toll-free number. Take advantage of any discounts you can muster. Hotels generally quote their highest rate first, so ask if there is an AAA discount, a senior rate, an AARP rate, a corporate rate, a military discount, or a frequent customer program, etc. Just keep asking and maybe, just maybe, the price will drop.

- At check-in, verify the hotel rate. Make sure it's still the lowest rate.
- Ask about weekly rates on accommodations and cars. Sometimes it's cheaper to rent by the week than by the day.
- If you're going to eat out, make sure you get a deal. Look at menus before you go. Many hotels and condo rental offices have a stack of restaurant menus, which can help you decide what you're in the mood for and that show the price range. Early-bird dinners are great, with restaurants offering incentives such as "buy-one, get-one-free" deals to get people in early. Go for it. It's the same food you'd pay double for a couple of hours later.
- Take advantage of the concierge or other services available wherever you are staying. Ask them where to find the deals, where a good reasonable place to eat might be, and where to get coupons or discounts.
- Always go to the visitor center when you arrive and load up on all the tourist material. Ask for coupons or current information on interesting (sometimes free) things to do.
- Shop at thrift stores and discounters for your souvenirs. You can almost always find great T-shirts with your vacation destination on them in Goodwill or Salvation Army stores. Or try Wal-Mart.
- Use a calling card, your credit card, or a pay telephone if you are making phone calls from a hotel that charges for direct-dial calls from your room.

 Tips: Travel

Linda Carter proposes a stay-at-home vacation; which you can do in a lot of cities, including her hometown of Nashville. Here is her example: "Before I went back to work full-time, our family of four, with girls ages seven and eight, could not afford a vacation. We had our vacation at home. We stayed at Carter's Motel (our home) and did fun things around Nashville each day." Her husband took the week off, and they took the following outings: Monday, they packed a lunch and went to the park, where they played on the playground and waded in the creek; Tuesday, they spent the day at a water park, taking their lunch; Wednesday, they went to the zoo; Thursday, they visited a histori-cal home; Friday, they went to an amusement park, using coupons to get in. They ate out each night and then came back to their "motel," ready to go the next day. They spent less than $200 and had a vacation that their family remembers as the best.

> According to the U.S. government the average American has less than $2,000 in savings. Think about that for a second. Every ten years, the average American earns about $200,000. Yet after expenses and taxes, there is only $2,000 left? How did this happen? One reason is that you've been conditioned to believe that spending money will make you happy.
>
> —Beardstown Ladies, from *Smart Spending for Big Savings*

Barbara Wise had a great idea for traveling with children: "Give each child a box of store-brand Band-Aids. They can spend a lot of time just opening the wrapping and finding places all over themselves and their car seats, dolls, teddy bears, or whatever to stick them on. You end up with a mess, but the quiet distraction is worth it." She also suggests children's books on tape from the library and individual tape players so each child can listen or play his or her own games.

"When traveling, I use the *Traveler Lodging Guide,* found at rest areas in most states. It contains coupons for hotels/motels across the state. I have found lodging for as little as $17.95. Most are well-known chains, and some offer a continental breakfast." —*Pam Barber*

"Check the local papers for churches or other organizations having fundraising suppers. The cost is usually $3 to $5. Bonus: You meet some wonderful people." —*Betty Wolfe*

"When going on vacation, rent a VCR camera instead of buying. Save hundreds." —*Billy Fiveash*

Pam Barber suggests that you contact the state department of tourism or city chamber of commerce for information on your destination. "You will mostly likely receive discounts, coupons, and useful information for your visit."

"Before going on a tour of two weeks or more where only one bag is allowed, I spray around the collar, sleeves, and fronts of blouses and jackets and the fronts and pocket areas of pants with Scotchguard or a fabric protector. This serves as a soil and water repellent, enabling me to wear a garment several times while on the trip." —*Eunice Doty*

To keep kids busy on long car trips, give each
child a box of store-brand Band-Aids.

"When searching for a motel or hotel, price shop. After finding a cheap rate, which in most cases are low-rate inns, don't be afraid to call a nicer motel or hotel and ask them to match the lowest rate you have found. You will be surprised that many will match rates, and you will have more amenities and a more deluxe room at the same cost." —*Jack Crouch*

"Last year, for spring break, we took a week-long vacation in Gatlinburg practically expense-free, thanks to time-share marketing. The companies put you in an area motel for free if you agree to listen to a one-to-two-hour presentation about their time-share condominiums. We planned three in a row of these. It was somewhat inconvenient to change motels every other day, but most of the companies also offered other freebies like a coupon book, show tickets, or meals at area restaurants. We were even offered $75 to listen to an additional presentation, which of course we did." —*Diana Kula*

> You should never skimp on brakes or parachutes.
> —*Savvy Discounts* newsletter

Joanne Bowman and her husband took an 8,000-mile, five-week trip in their family car. The couple stayed in moderately priced motels but curbed costs by cooking most of their own food. "No way I could eat restaurant meals for five weeks, so we took along a Koolatron cooler/warmer, a small portable refrigerator that plugs into the cigarette lighter. It can also be used to keep foods warm by flipping the switch. It sits neatly in the backseat, secured by a seat belt (the coolers range from $65 to $115). We took it into the room at night and used a twelve-volt adapter plugged into a wall outlet. We also took a small ice chest, which we filled from motel ice machines, to store our soft drinks. For cooking, I took an electric hot pot about the size of a percolator to boil water. It worked great for boiling corn on the cob, potatoes in their jackets, fresh asparagus, and eggs, as well as soups. I took three fondue pots with alcohol burners (two of which I had bought at yard sales for $2 each) to use at picnic areas. A small skillet sits neatly on the stand for cooking meats, sausages, eggs, etc. Isopropyl alcohol is cheap, goes a long way, and burns hot. It's also good for disinfecting the motel vanity before and after cooking. We took a starter supply of groceries from home and shopped for groceries along the way with coupons I had clipped from the newspaper. On our next trip, I plan to take a George Foreman Grill and possibly a small Crockpot, so that the next day's pot can cook overnight while I sleep."

> The key is to keep short-term wants from taking priority over long-term needs.
>
> —Ginger Applegarth, from *The Money Diet*

"When we travel, we always pack a cooler with cans or small bottles of soft drinks purchased on sale at supermarkets at home. We carry extra so that when one is removed from the cooler, it is replaced. Before leaving the hotel, we re-ice and restock the cooler." —*Jack Crouch*

8

Saving Wherever You Can

Sometimes it is the little things that count—because the little scraps of savings add up to big amounts of money. Being cheap or frugal is really a mind-set, a case of evaluating your purchases before you make them, of being resourceful whenever and wherever you can. Then (ideally) when you add it all up, you will have something to show for your smart-money habits.

I'm starting with a list of money-saving suggestions from the Tennessee Agricultural Extension Service. This list touches on a wide variety of areas for potential savings. Then I look at ideas for saving on automobiles, prescriptions, and more.

Here are some smart ideas from the Tennessee Agricultural Extension Service:

- Cook from scratch to cut down on the purchase of convenience foods.

- Grow a garden if possible.
- Use dry or evaporated milk for cooking instead of more expensive fresh whole milk.
- Use cooked cereals instead of more expensive sugar-coated dry ones.
- Plan your own redecorating, using items on hand. Look for free classes on budget decorating, and take advantage of information in magazines and books.
- Carry only replacement value insurance on your house or car.
- Use glasses instead of paper cups.
- Learn to barter with neighbors and friends for things such as home repairs or fresh vegetables.
- Carpool when possible.
- Carefully plan the use of the car to reduce the amount of driving.
- Inventory each family member's wardrobe to determine which items must be replaced or added.
- Try to develop an attitude in children that hand-me-down clothing is economical, is less wasteful, and can be enjoyable.
- Sew as much as is practical.
- Investigate services offered by local health departments, public school clinics, and immunization centers.
- Ask the druggist to fill prescriptions by generic name, if your doctor recommends it. Never take drugs prescribed to another person.
- Use the public library, mobile library, or local college or university library for reading materials. This can help you reduce the number of magazine and newspaper subscriptions.

- Make gifts instead of buying them.
- Give services instead of gifts, such as adult-sitting, baby-sitting, house-watching, and pet-sitting.
- If you need legal services, contact Legal Aid for help.
- Do activities that cost only minimal amounts of money, such as hiking, picnicking, visiting a museum or library, or attending free concerts.
- Consider the cost of habits such as smoking and drinking alcoholic beverages.
- Take vacations at home. Do something special every day.
- Have potlucks at home for family and friends. This way everyone shares in the food costs.
- Attend high school or even sandlot sports events instead of more expensive college or professional athletic events.

The experts call it "living within your income." I call it smart!

Tips: Automobiles

"Of course, buy cars used. Take good care of your car." —*Mary Carter*

"Look for church, charity, or school car washes to get a good car wash for $3 to $5 instead of what you might pay at a professional wash." —*Bob Battle*

"To remove heavy frost and light ice from my car windshield and windows, I buy windshield washer de-icing fluid and put it into a spray bottle to use. At about $2 a gallon, it is much cheaper and lasts longer than those aerosol cans and works well for most conditions." —*Richard Cotham*

"When it comes to automobile maintenance, we check a lot of things, like oil, tires, batteries, and brakes, but how many of us check our automobile insurance coverage? Insurance premiums go up every year while the value of our vehicles goes down. We pay more and get less. Call your agent. Request that your insurance premium be adjusted to the value of your car. Our call gained us a savings of close to $250 a year on one auto. If your agent does not want to give you an estimated value of what they would give you if your car were totaled, get a quote from one of the companies advertised on TV or on the Internet. Save big bucks. Make a phone call!" —*Del and Lex Tinsley*

"If you have to park your car in the hot sun and don't have a folding sun shield to cover your windshield, grab the large road atlas or map from your glove compartment and fit it to the windshield. Turn down the sun visors to keep the map in place. Presto, your car will be cool and comfortable when you return!" —*Karla Brown*

Debra Bryant says using a GM credit card has netted her more than $1,800 in rebates toward a new GM car. Since she pays her bill in full each month, she isn't paying interest, but accumulating bucks for her next car. The point here is to select a credit card that rewards you where you want to be rewarded. She also takes advantage of offers to test-drive cars for gifts or money. For test-driving an Intrigue, she got a $100 savings bond. For checking out a Monte Carlo, she got a $90 camera outfit. For sampling a Saturn, she got an on-line gift certificate to landsend.com. She also takes all the credit card companies up on their introductory offers and gets gifts and gift certificates to Red Lobster and other places and then cancels the cards.

Liz Schneider got her idea from her husband's ninety-seven-year-old grandmother, who would wait until it rained and drive her car out of the carport and into the rain for a free car wash. "I took her idea a step further. When it rains, I leave my car out, dress in a big overcoat and hat (more as a disguise than protection), get a bucket of soapy water, and run a soapy rag over the car. The car is wetted and rinsed by Mother Nature, and the finish is protected from those automatic car washes."

> Use our easy credit plan. One hundred percent down, nothing to pay each month.
> —Sign seen in store window by a reader of the *Tightwad Gazette*

"Instead of paying big bucks on automobile security for 'the Club,' buy a short chain and a good padlock." —*Billy Fiveash*

"When you go to the tire store to have your tires rotated, ask if you can have one of the old truck inner tubes that hasn't rotted. Cut the tubes crosswise in one-half- to one-inch strips, and you have very large rubber bands. Loop several of them together for even longer bands when you need one to go around something really big. They cost nothing and are a lot cheaper than bungee cords." —*Wayne King*

"My father likes the way brand-new windshield wiper blades keep the windshield clear, so he replaces his often. But instead of changing out both, he puts a new one on the driver's side and moves the driver's side one to the passenger side. He has to buy a new set of blades only every other time." —*Martha Brinson*

"Before turning the gasoline pump on, I place the nozzle into the gas tank, raise the hose as high as possible, and then open up the nozzle. You would be surprised at how much gas is in the hose and then in my tank. Then I turn on the pump and pump my gas. When the tank is full, I turn off the pump and raise the hose again to get the remaining gas in the hose." —*Grover Hastings*

Don't start your engines until you're ready to roll. "During these days of high gasoline prices, I see many people get in their car and immediately start up their engines. Then they attach their seat belt, straighten their clothes, arrange their belongings, etc." Doing this before starting up would save some cold cash, says "Slim Jim" Murray, who estimates that if you waste fifteen to thirty seconds each time you get in the car, you could be talking about as much as "three to six hours of time in a year that your car just sits there wasting gas and money."

"When a gas station has a free car wash with an eight-gallon fill-up, I fill up to only eight gallons, even if I am on empty. That way, my car can go through the free wash more often." —*Lynn Yuchnitz*

Tips: Correspondence

Rebecca Honey Graham makes her own postcards. "You can make them out of cereal boxes, cracker boxes, and other boxes that you have in your kitchen and normally throw away. You are saving money and doing your part to recycle."

Robert Meyer and his brother have had fun being cheap and sending the same birthday card back and forth year after year, with each brother simply initialing it and dating it. "It was not originally meant to be cheap, but we are still sending each other the same card and have saved not only a lot of money, but also a lot of time looking for the right card."

"Give your husband the same birthday card each year. He will never know." —*Mary Nell Paris*

"Let me preface this by saying I have never done this because it's too cheap. But my husband's barber gave him a cheap idea for Valentine's Day. He and his wife go out to dinner (probably a cheap place) and then after dinner they choose a romantic store like Kmart, Wal-Mart, or maybe a drugstore. Then they walk hand in hand to the card aisle. They quietly give each other about five minutes to find the perfect card and then they look into each other's eyes, give the mate the chosen card, and maybe even read it to each other. They kiss, put the card back on the shelf, and say 'Happy Valentine's Day!' They saved about $5." —*Leigh Ann Anderson*

"Sidewalk chalk can do the walk," says Ruth Ward, who uses sidewalk chalk for all of her public messages. "Chalk your designs on the street: 'Happy Birthday James' or 'garage sale' or 'newlyweds.' It's fun, especially if you get the kids involved."

"We married during the Depression, and for holidays and birthdays we verbally exchanged wishes. Then as our finances improved, we purchased romantic and expensive cards for each occasion. I saved each and every one. One year, I suggested that my husband might like to shop for a card from my collection. The idea was a winner. Each holiday he carefully chose the one he thought most fitting. I was as thrilled with his selection as I could be—much more so than if he had spent time and money buying a new one." —Iola Watkins

Jolana Boyd makes her own note cubes by cutting scrap paper to the same size, stacking them in a pile, and painting one edge of the stack with rubber cement.

"I needed to make money stretch for my wedding, so I cut corners on a few things. For my RSVP cards, I got some postcards from the post office that had the postage already on them. Then I ordered rubber stamps from an office supply store. One stamp was my name and address, which I also used with gold ink on the outside of the invitation for my return address. I stamped that in black on the postage side of the postcard, and then for the other side, I got a rubber stamp that had "please RSVP before . . ." and then had them write their name and how many would be attending. I invested only about $16 in the rubber stamps, and the postcards cost only a penny plus the amount of the postage. And I can use the address rubber stamp again." —*Ellen Goebel*

"When you receive mail, cut out the printed part with your name and address. It can be used as a return address label when paying bills like light, phone, and cable." —*Tommy Abood*

"Use postcards instead of greeting cards."
   —Linda Shelton

M. Collins suggests making note cards out of invitations and notices you receive. "Just write the notes on the blank side."

Tips: Telephone Calls

"To save money on long distance calls, turn your recorder or voice mail off when you go out of town or on vacation. That way you won't have to return calls of people who called while you were away." —*Karen Pirtle*

"When leaving on a trip, I have an understanding with someone at home that I will call when I arrive at my destination; I call person-to-person, asking for myself. This lets the person at home know that I have arrived safely and—guess what?—no phone bill." —*Marie Jett*

"I am a real estate agent. However, I refuse to put up with the high cost and constant annoyance of a cell phone. I do wear a pager, though, and when I am beeped, I stop at the nearest pay phone." —*John Rickman* (He says he carries plenty of change to call the office or clients.)

"I seldom, if ever, make long-distance calls and was getting frustrated to find nearly $20 charged to my phone bill each month for access fees, extra phone fees, federal and state taxes, and so on. My solution: I called my long-distance carrier (AT&T) and asked them to cancel my long-distance service. I called my local carrier (BellSouth) and requested that they put a freeze on my phone so that no long-distance calls could be made. I then purchased a prepaid AT&T long-distance calling card for $10, which gives me forty-five minutes of long-distance time. There are no additional charges, and I can call long distance from my home or anywhere I choose, without paying the additional surcharges normally charged by the long-distance carrier." —*Jack Williams*

Tips: Wardrobe

"Buy all men's socks and women's knee highs the same color, and when one is worn out or lost, you will still have good matched socks. This also saves time because you do not to have to match socks every time you put them on." —*Bill Turner*

Robert Anderson cleverly resoled his worn Teva sandals with roadside treasure: "I found a chunk of tire from a blowout that had some tread left. I separated it one steel belt at a time, with a set of pliers. Then using a utility knife, I cut the tire into the shape of a Teva sole, using the sandals as templates. After buying a $2.99 tube of Goop adhesive, I glued the 'new soles' (old tire) in place and clamped them to dry." He then had to replace the Velcro fasteners on the straps, and his all-terrain sandals were as good as new. "Instead of buying a new pair for $45, I invested in a tube of glue and some Velcro, and have sandals that are good for another 50,000 miles."

"Purchase a can of Krylon spray paint in a beige color and spray paint your shoes. For only $3.50 (at most hardware stores), you can make them look like new again. If you get bored with the color, invest in several cans of various colors and have a new pair of shoes at a very cheap price." — *Deborah Hutchison*

"Make a poncho out of your shower curtain or shower curtain liner." —*the "Cheap Creep"*

"Cover your ironing board with aluminum foil and then cover with an ironing board cover. The heat reflects off the aluminum foil so that you don't have to iron both sides." —*Lynn Yuchnitz*

"I carry a fabric dryer sheet in my purse. Not only does my purse smell great, but the sheet is wonderful when my dress or slacks cling to my panty hose. I just rub one up and down, and presto, no more cling!" —*Betty Wolfe*

"I wear a lot of cotton clothes, and after a while, they look faded.

About once a year, I put all my black garments in the washing machine with some black liquid dye (two bottles). Everything comes out looking brand-new, and all the garments are the same shade of black." — *Elizabeth Schneider*

"Need a garment bag? Just use your coat by putting it 'on' the clothes you are taking on your trip and button it up. Works great!" —*Colleen Jones*

"I'm a little old lady who likes to wear hats, especially to church on Sunday. I make hats or often redecorate them to match my outfit. One friend told me the most fascinating hat I wear is one I created. For the funeral of a loved one, I was given a pot of flowers in a straw basket. I put the basket on my head upside down, turned the edges up for a brim, put a pink band around it, and walked out in a beautiful cool-looking summer hat. It's beauty parlors that ruined the hat market, but I don't wear a beauty parlor hairdo." —*Virginia Naylor Smith*

"Stick to the basic colors, and mix and match for your wardrobe. Hit sales and discount stores to do this." —*Elaine Newcomb*

"A good way to keep white leather tennis shoes sparkling clean is to clean them with Tilex shower cleaner." —*Carolyn Puckett*

"Buy more than one pair of el cheapo one-size-fits-all mittens in the same color, so if one is lost, you still have a pair that matches." —*Nina Nissen*

"I work in an office and wear panty hose daily. Panty hose is expensive, so I economize by cutting off a leg with a run in it and saving the panty with the good leg attached. Once I accumulate two, I have a new set of hose to wear and save money." —*Carrie Cowan*

"Make your own insoles. Take a foam meat tray from the grocery store, put your foot on it, and trace around it. Cut out with scissors and insert in shoe." —*Billy Fiveash*

"When I buy a dress or suit and can't seem to find that pair of earrings that match exactly, I make my own. Most suits have a couple of extra self-covered buttons attached. I buy a package of earring backs (six in a pack) at Wal-Mart in the crafts department and glue them on the back of the buttons. They are a perfect match, and I have received many compliments on them." —*Joyce Henderson*

"When shopping, I find that clothes are cheaper in the men's department. So when I am looking for jogging clothes, sweaters, flannel shirts, or jackets, I check there first." —*Dianne Gregory*

"Don't buy clothes in their current season. Why pay top dollar for something that will cost 50 percent less in a couple of months?" —*Mary Carter*

Christy Henley says instead of buying garment bags for covering off-season clothes, just use old pillowcases: "You simply cut holes in the top and slip them over the hangers."

Mary Stephens knows how to save on house slippers: "I wear the pretty flat ones with the open backs. Since the heel part seems to get soiled and worn out first, I put strips of Scotch tape across the back to protect them. These strips can then be pulled off anytime I want."

Shop in the children's section of discount or department stores for the popular little purses. "They are lightweight and come in all colors, and the best thing is that you can fit in a compact, brush, lipstick, identification, coins and bills, and even a small phone or pager, all for $1.99 to $4.99. You can put it over your shoulder and dance."—*Ruth Ward*

> Money makes money and the money that money makes, makes more money.
> —Benjamin Franklin

Tennis enthusiast John Nixon found a place that will resole tennis shoes for $18 a pair. It's Athletic Shoe Repair, 2901 S. Main St., Santa Ana, CA 92707. He says the cost is only $16 a pair if you have four pair or more. "The shoes are already broken in, and of course, the leather tops remain in good condition for the second time around."

Virginia Small keeps her white leather shoes looking nice this way: "I cover the scuff marks with one or two light brushings of Liquid Paper (yes, correction fluid), letting dry after each application. After the scuff mark is covered to my satisfaction, I polish the shoe with my favorite paste polish, let it dry thoroughly, and then shine with a soft cloth. My white leather shoes look like new."

"After two or three months of wear from your athletic shoes, check the soles; if they have blown out, return for an exchange or refund. Many manufacturers will allow a return or exchange if requested in a timely manner." —*Shera Goode*

"To protect clothes on hangers, use a large garbage bag or shopping bag. Flatten the bag, and place a piece of duct tape on the midpoint of the seam. Then cut a half moon to make a circle, the size a hanger goes through. If it is not a clear bag, take a marker and write on the outside what garment is in there." —*Carolyn Spann*

The new "illusion" necklaces, costume jewelry costing $10 to $30, are simply monofilament line plus pendants. Shirley Phipps suggests using nylon fishing line to make your own jewelry out of charms and orphaned earrings.

"I used to wear white bras under most things, wearing dark bras only when white showed through. Now I do just the opposite— wear dark bras (black, green, burgundy, etc.) with everything and wear white only when I need to. I get longer wear out of the dark bras because they don't turn gray." —*Lynn Yuchnitz*

"Have a run in your hose? Stop the run with a glue stick. It works like nail polish." —*Lynn Yuchnitz*

Tips: If You Can Sew, You Can Save

"When your knit jogging suits are worn or faded, cut the best sleeve or leg off. Sew a piece of elastic in both the top and the bottom of whichever you select. At the top, attach a loop for a hanger. Hang under the counter near the sink and stuff your empty plastic grocery bags in it. You can remove them either from the top or bottom." —Joe Powell

"For folks who sew, the best buy in town for unusual buttons is at your local thrift store. You can find marvelous buttons on garments that cost half as much as what you'd pay for just the buttons at a sewing store." —*Michelle Ann Sabine*

"Use a free magnet upside down on your sewing table to keep pins and needles in place." —*Alice Huang*

"When rehemming a skirt, sleeves, or pants legs, I carefully find the end of the chain stitch usually used. Again, carefully, I rewind the thread on a spool or toilet paper roll as I unravel the hem thread. If it is extremely kinked, I dampen it ever so slightly with wet fingers. Usually it straightens itself out nicely just by being rolled tight. When the thread is dry, I reuse it to rehem the garment. Not only does this save me a bit of thread, which is negligible, but it saves me time in shopping for thread to match the garment, and usually the original thread is a closer match than I could buy, anyway." —*Claire Minie*

Margarette Brown makes her husband's ties: "After fifty-three years of marriage, he has accumulated lots. I am ripping some of them up and making me some vests."

Margarette Brown makes her husband's ties. "After fifty-three years of marriage, he has accumulated lots."

"Learn to mend your own clothes and dry clean rarely." —*Mary Carter*

Pamela Chandler recycled her husband's dress shirts with worn collars. "I cut out twelve eighteen-by-eighteen-inch squares from the backs of the shirt material, which was in good condition. I made a fold and machine-stitched the hem, and, voilà, beautiful restaurant-quality napkins!"

"Sew all hard-to-stay-on buttons with dental floss. They never come off." —*Donna Burns*

"Use sheets for curtains instead of buying fabric."
—*Beulah Mitchell*

"At prom time, get your dress at Goodwill and alter it yourself. You can make it any way you want, and you will save hundreds of dollars." —*Jamie Streeter*

"I make a lot of quilts, so I buy clothes, blankets, and pillowcases cheap, and then I don't have that much money invested in the quilt, if I want to sell it." —*Rosie Mitchell*

"You can take bed ruffles and make curtains. First, cut the ruffle in half and seam it up, and you have a very cheap pair of curtains." —*Marie Bush*

 Tips: Prescriptions

"When given a prescription for a new drug, I often find that it doesn't agree with me. I ask the druggist for a smaller amount to see if I can tolerate it. Better yet, I ask the doctor for a sample, if available." —*Gloria Fishbein*

"Get into research programs if you qualify. I just entered a six-year high blood pressure program. My medication will be free during this time." —*Christine Green*

9

Websites and Miscellaneous Tips

Good Websites for Cheapos

The Internet is clearly a resource that cheapos are going to be using more and more to save money and comparison shop. This section offers a mere sampling and is included just to get you started, if you are not already surfing for bargains. It includes some of the Websites that cheap readers have recommended to me. But the best way to get into this is to try a few sites and then just experiment. Happy hunting!

Some of the most often recommended cheap sites are www.kroger.com, where you can get coupons (primarily for Kroger products), and www.valupage.com, where you can download software and print out sheets to take to your grocery to get "webbucks," or rebates for buying certain products. Others include www.stuff.com, www.smartsource.com, www.coolsavings.com, www.hotcoupons.com, www.centsoff.com, www.coupons.com, www.freeshop.com, www.save.com, and www.mysimon.com, which is a comparison pricing service. Another site, www.bargainflicks.com, lists all sorts of coupons for about twenty different on-line retailers. "Lots of good offers," says Daryl Brown.

For travel, go to www.travelocity.com, www.lowestfare.com, www.cheaptickets.com, or any of the airline sites and look for deals. Others to check are www.expedia.com and, of course, www.priceline.com, where you name your own price on airline tickets and hotel rooms.

> Money will not make you happy, and happy will not make you money.
> —Groucho Marx

Lots of readers have suggested the www.dialpad.com site to place phone calls for free. "All you need is a microphone and speakers hooked up to your computer," says Esther Ford. "The party you call answers the phone, and you talk on the computer microphone and hear from your computer speakers. It's free."

"AddAll.com is a book-searching and comparison Website," says Daryl Brown. "It will search more than forty on-line book retailers for the best price. It calculates the shipping charges to your home address and the sales tax, if any. Combine this search engine with a coupon from www.bargainflicks.com, and you can get items really cheap."

For greeting cards, check out www.bluemountain.com, www.123-greetings.com, www.cardmaster.com, and www.ElectronicPostcards.com, says Carol Borhman.

There's a treasure trove of bargains and information out there. One of Jennifer Good's favorite sites is www.freebitz.com, which has free stuff

The Internet is clearly a resource that cheapos are going to be using more and more to save money.

and coupons. Check out auction sites like eBay.com, ubid.com, and bid.com, which are popular with readers. Get stuff free with rebates from www.CyberRebate.com. Go on-line to sites like www.1aboutfreestuff.com and www.sassysue.com for free samples. If you have children who are reading or to whom you're reading, visit the National Education Association's "Read Across America" Webpage for a list of one hundred favorite books selected by kids and teachers across the country. The site is www.nea.org/readacross. Then, of course, you can go to the library and check them out.

Some other Web ideas from readers follow.

> Remember that
> credit is money.
> —Benjamin Franklin

Tips: Websites

Chris Ferrell writes that helpnetworks.com "is a shopping site that allows on-line shoppers to designate a portion of every purchase to the school or nonprofit agency of their choice. Visitors can choose from more than fifty on-line retailers, and as long as the shopper comes through the helpnetworks portal, a portion of their gross purchase (5 percent on average) will be donated to the cause they have designated." Ferrell says it's a Nashville-based company dedicated to harnessing the power of the Internet to build community and improve education.

Another reader recommends www.beauty.com, a beauty Website that offered her a $10 gift certificate good on her first order.

"If you've had a baby in the last twelve months, visit www.ringling. com/onstage/babies/babies.htm to get a free ticket to the Greatest Show on Earth. This free ticket has no expiration date and can be redeemed at any time in your child's life," says Carolyn Jernigan.

Debra Bryant joined www.mypoints.com and www.freeride.com. "For surfing forty-five minutes or fewer daily, I have earned points that can be converted into gift certificates: $25 in Bass Pro gift certificates, $25 in Red Lobster gift certificates. I almost have the number of points needed to get a $50 Cabela's gift certificate."

Stephanie Smith is also a fan of www.mypoints.com, saying she and her brother have gotten points for visiting Websites and redeemed them for gift certificates at Target, Eddie Bauer, and Chili's.

Duane Karvonen and C. J. Joshlin wanted people to know about www.thehungersite.com, where you can click once a day to have food donated to the hungry.

For an on-line bargain-hunter's paradise, go to www.outletzoo.com, says Carrie McAleese.

Jim Rupert called to say his favorite Website is www.egghead.com, where he bought a digital camera (Sony 88) he had seen at retail for $900. He paid $638, with no tax and no shipping. He also bought a treadmill for a third off retail, without shipping or tax.

Michele Friedrichsen said www.freebies.com is "incredible. You get free food, recipes, perfume, cosmetics, CDs. The gifts are endless, usually for just filling out a survey.

Tom DeRamus makes free long-distance phone calls by signing up at www.broadpoint.com. He also sends free faxes at www.fax4free.com.

Tips: Miscellaneous Ways to Save

Some tips just don't quite fit into neat little categories or chapters, so here are some more great and clever tips. (Some of my favorite tips are in this section!)

"If your costume jewelry has tarnished, don't throw it out. Clean with equal parts of mayonnaise and catsup. Apply and wipe away quickly. If not clean, repeat." —*Kathryn Groover*

"Saturday is my day off, and I have numerous errands to run. I organize my errands on paper in the order that I would arrive at them while driving, getting the things done on the right side of the road as I go and on the left as I come home. I have all my coupons in the order that I will use them (post office, dry cleaners, grocery store, department store, etc.). I make sure I am aware of specials that grocery stores have in the area I am driving in, so I can run in and pick up specials and save bucks. Plus I save on gas since I never backtrack, because I have organized and planned my stops in the order I reach them." —*Patricia Rickman*

"'Waste not want not' is my mother-in-law's motto. When the dentist replaced my father-in-law's four gold crowns with porcelain crowns, he brought them home and presented them to Lucy. Not one to let anything, especially gold, go to waste, she had the crowns melted down and made into a nugget that she proudly wears around her neck. When anyone comments on the necklace, she is thrilled to give the history behind the unusual jewelry." —*Carolyn Gregory*

Mary Ann Liden has a host of good ideas, including buying antique furniture, joining AAA if you travel, having $50 a month drafted out of your account into a no-load mutual fund, swapping baby-sitting with other families, and starting a coupon exchange.

"Spend your money the three days after payday the same way you spend it the three days before payday, and it will stretch much further." —*Joan Greenwood*

Wilma Simpson keeps her plastic grocery bags in a Pringles can in her trunk for all kinds of uses. "If I buy a plant, I can pull out a bag and keep from messing up the trunk."

"For my wedding I went to several different Goodwill thrift stores and bought different-sized brass candlestick holders. In all, I spent about $37 on about fifty candlestick holders. Then, since they were rather tarnished, I spray painted them gold, which actually looked cooler than the brass. I got taper candles at Old Time Pottery for a great price, and instead of flowers on the table at the reception, we had different-sized candles and can use them again." —*Ellen Goebel*

"Admit your age if it will save you money." —*Eleanor Barrett*

"Always bring your self-stick address labels when you will need to fill out applications, like at the Women's Show." —*Linda Cantrell*

"Always have enough cash flow to be able to take advantage of sales and specials. Stock up. Buy as much as you can. This may mean some extra short-term expense as you spend more at the store than planned. But in the long run, it can mean substantial savings when done regularly." —*Bill Hennessee*

> They that go a-borrowing, go a-sorrowing.
>
> —John Clarke

"Find a way to save $10 a week—double coupons, brown-bag lunch for a day or two, trim your long-distance calls, etc. Just find a way. What can you do with $10 a week? One year, $520, buy a new set of tires; two years, $1,040, pay cash for Christmas gifts and receive no bills in January; three years, $1,560, pay off credit cards; four years, $2,080, finance your vacation. Set your goal, and you will be rewarded!" —*Imogene Norris*

"In the past year, my salary was drastically reduced and I often found myself with no money. I discovered that I could walk through the drive-through lanes at fast food restaurants and find change: pennies, nickels, dimes, and quarters. The most I have found at one time is 75¢. If I went through two or three times, I often got enough for a drink or a burger." —*Missy Willoughby*

"For my husband's office, we take paper copied on one side, cut each sheet into four pieces, stack several sheets together, and staple. Place by the phone and we are ready to take messages." —*Deborah Irvin*

"If you love to watch the yellow finches gather around your feeders, place an aluminum deli tray at the bottom of your feeder. It will save you money by catching the seeds the birds drop as they peck the seeds from the feeders." —*Jack and Inez Riley*

"Know when to pay your bills. Gas and electric bills carry heavy penalties for late payments, unlike the phone bill. If you can't pay before the due date, wait until the billing cycle almost ends and send the check. In this way, you have use of the money, and the effective rate is reduced over the thirty days." —*David Broemel*

"Look for free things that have been discarded or lost alongside the road. I'm not advocating dumpster diving, although that is a great way to find and salvage goods. The concept is just to keep your eyes open as you drive the interstates or secondary roads. Just this week, I found a nine-foot tie-down strap and a VW hubcap. Not too long ago, I found a cell phone, a sheet of 3/4-inch plywood, and a pair of pliers. The best idea of all is to combine roadside scavenging with daily runs or bicycle rides. Bikes are best because you can easily cover twenty miles or more at one time. You will stay in shape and be able to fill your tool box for free, all at the same time." —*David Broemel*

"Maintain a no-fee checking account." —*Stacy Harris*

"My family and I use those great little plastic (black or clear) film canisters that you usually throw away after getting film developed for everything—saving pennies, dimes, nickels, and quarters; storing safety pins; storing jewelry in a suitcase; organizing items in drawers. They are also great for placing in your purse for any small item you don't want to lose! The uses are endless." —*Caroline Holley*

"My husband is so cheap that he sometimes gets the newspaper out of the recycle bin instead of buying me one." —*Paula McMahan*

"My husband-to-be and I are having several aunts escorted in during the beginning of the marriage ceremony. We wanted to purchase them each a corsage, but they were $6 and up. We decided to give them each a single rose, with a ribbon around it. They will carry the rose as they are escorted to their seat. This cost only $2 each. You could probably get an even better deal on a carnation." —*Tanya Mathews*

"To get rid of flies, get your upright vacuum cleaner out and take the hose and hold it up and zap the flies into the hose. It really works." —*Ginger Smith*

"Use it up, wear it out, make it do, or do without." —*a favorite quote of Mary Rorick*

"When I buy anything in a zippered bag (dust ruffle, sheet, etc.), I save the bags. I use them to store letters, pictures, and so on, for my bulletin boards in my classroom. The materials are enclosed and easy to see and find, and will stay clean too." —*Judy Anderson*

"To offset some of our monthly costs and enable me to stay home with our new baby, we elected to buy a duplex instead of a single-family home. Every month, we get a check totaling over half of our mortgage payment, not to mention some wonderful tax advantages." —*Jenah Friend*

"If you are overpaying dues at a health club, drop your membership. Buy some good shoes and hit the road." —*Mary Carter*

Dee Weisbarth says one of her best money-savers is taking advantage of the four-day work week. "My work day begins at 7 A.M. and ends at 5:45 P.M. Tuesday through Friday. I have saved fifty-four miles round trip per week wear and tear on my car, plus gas expenses. Over a year's time, I have noticed an added bonus of less stress in my life, more flexibility on weekends (giving me lots more time to hit the garage sales), and of course the time to bake bread. I plan meals on Monday to carry me through the next four days."

Jolana Boyd says she had trouble finding an earring tree and came up with a good solution. "I bought a piece of plastic canvas from a craft store and ran a ribbon between the two corners for hanging. It works great for both post and dangling earrings. The canvas comes in a variety of colors and can be cut into any shape."

Linda Walker gives new meaning to "Christmas in July": "Once school gets out, my children and I go to lots of yard sales. During the month of June, we collect as many Christmas items that are cheap and like new as we can. Then in July or August, we have a 'Christmas in July (or August)' sale with the items we collected. We usually make $500 to $600 for a two-day sale (about 75 percent of this money is profit). We set this money aside for gifts at Christmas."

"A few years ago when we built our home, the painter suggested that he take the leftover paint from other rooms in the house and mix them all together and paint the inside of the garage. The idea sounded a little crazy, but we said go ahead. It worked out fine. From light blue, beige, and another color or so, we got a nice shade of green." —Joe Dillon

To repair decorative picture frames, "spread chewed-up bubble gum on places that need repairing. Stick it on and shape to the desired design. Let harden a week or two and then spray with gold paint. Beautiful." —Helen B. Coker

To fight ants, "simply sprinkle some instant grits right out of the box on an ant hill and just sit back and watch. This will work only with uncooked, dry, instant grits. All activity in the hive will cease within a day or less. I am told that the queen ant ingests one of the grits and then explodes. I have not actually seen this happen, but I know that it works. Not only are grits cheaper than ant poison, they are much friendlier for the environment." —*Lance McKerley*

"Call Discount Bridal Service's toll-free number (1-800-874-8794) to find a local rep, who can help you buy your dream dress for less. DBS can also supply dresses for attendants or prom goers at great prices, too. Their Website is http://www.discountbridalservice.com/." —*Susan Poulter*

"My husband does all of our mechanic work. He buys his name-brand tools for 50 to 80 percent off retail at pawn shops. I buy videos of our favorite movies for $4 to $5 each at pawn shops, too. Our teenagers buy their CDs at pawn shops. They cost about 75 percent less than at music stores." —*Donna King*

"Afraid of someone going through your trash and getting your credit card and other information, but you're not up to paying for an expensive paper shredder? Well, place your mail containing such information in a large plastic bag and dump the cat litter contents into the bag. Anyone who opens the bag will close it immediately and will never want to thumb through your mail." —*Jerrod Daniels*

"Before buying a new product, see if someone has it and will let you try a sample before buying it. Perhaps you will find out that you don't like it." —*Nadyne Petty*

"Cheap people always refill their water bottles, but really cheap people refill them at public drinking fountains." —*Sophia Absar*

"Don't throw away that old Frisbee. Make three holes around the rim and insert wire and hang from a tree branch or post. Fill with birdseed or water. It can also be used as a pet dish." —*Dorothy Westin*

"Ever wonder what you could do with those cardboard bathroom tissue rolls and all that lint that comes out of your dryer? You stuff those rolls full of lint, and use them to start camp fires or fires in your fireplace in the winter." —*Faye Washington*

"For my physical fitness exercise, instead of buying weights, I tie five pounds of rocks in a bag at each end of a broomstick and away I go lifting. I am now ninety and going strong." —*Virginia Naylor Smith*

Before you consult your fancy, consult your purse.
—Benjamin Franklin

"I could suggest many tips on saving a dollar here or a few quarters there, but here is the best thing I have ever done to save money: Last year we refinanced our home loan to a lower interest rate and switched from a thirty-year mortgage to a fifteen-year mortgage. For only $30 dollars more a month we will be able to save almost $100,000 on our house payments. We plan to use those savings to help with our kids' college expenses. Was it hard to scrape up the refinancing fee? Yes, but the payoff is so great." —*Ken Hutchison*

"I have discovered that the small bubble wrap makes a very good toe cushion for ingrown toenails and nails about to fall off. Simply cut small strips and place around the painful nail," positioning it before you put on panty hose or socks. —*Dot Ussery*

"I keep a supply of all colors of felt-tipped markers and use them for any number of repair jobs around the house (everything from a ceramic wreath that was chipped to a painted basket that had a nick in it to a figurine and earring)." —*Virginia Small*

"I take my daily junk mail and cut out my name and address and use as address labels and for labels on items, such as dishes taken to potluck dinners and books on loan. There are any number of uses for the labels, which some people shred before throwing away their junk mail." —*Barbara Thompson*

"I travel from time to time and sometimes get out of my banking area. I hate paying those stupid ATM fees ($2 to $3), so I go to a Wal-Mart, Target, Kroger, etc. Then I pick up a pack of gum, usually the small Wrigley pack that's priced at 25¢, and buy it with my ATM (debit) card. When the scan machine or cashier asks if I want cash back, I get my money and a pack of gum. At least I get something in return, and I have fresh breath also." —*Joel Thacker*

"I use the bags from the dry cleaner as trash bags. I tie a knot in the end that has the small hole for the hangers and they work great. I never buy trash bags." —*Dan Boone*

"If you need a heating pad and don't own one or can't get the plug to reach the socket, try this: Take a medium or large baking potato with the skin on it and microwave it for one and a half minutes. Carefully take it out of the microwave and wrap in a damp washcloth or put it inside an old sock and tie it with a twist tie. It will be very hot and will retain heat for thirty minutes, unlike a hot water bottle. I don't eat it afterward, though. This really works—I use it on my forehead for my sinuses." —*Carol Bohrman*

"Instead of using a level, use a clear measuring cup filled with water. Place on object to be leveled and see if the line of water is even. Adjust object until water level is even on the measuring cup." —*Dorinda Gaw*

"Keep life simple. If I didn't need it five years ago, why do I need it now? The more I have, the more I have to keep up and maintain." —*James Calvin Buckner*

"You can use newspaper bags to put over your cast when you have a broken arm and you can't take a shower. Just tuck the end of the bag down inside the cast and it will stay pretty dry." —*Pam Thomason*

"Many photo-processing services will refund the price of any developed picture you don't like. When you get your pictures back, sort through them, choose those you don't want (blurry, too light, too dark, etc.), and return them. You can get as much as 33¢ back for each one." —*Corine Sandifer*

"Buy wide rubber bands and cut in two to make more." —*Bill Turner*

"Educate yourself about quality. Only buy name brands when quality is superior to store brands and generics. It's always a better value to wear something you like often than something cheap never." —*Mary Carter*

"I have attended insurance and financial seminars in which I was under no obligation to buy anything. At all of these, my husband and I enjoyed a delicious buffet meal out, and at two of them, I also received a free cookbook. My husband got the cookbooks, too, so I gave those to one of our daughters. Never turn down a survey. Over the last years I have received a large-beam flashlight, a camera, a set of steak knives, an atlas, an address book, a boom box, and money ranging from a few dollars up to $50." —*Linda Rivers*

Cathy Conrad says to be sure you are getting the corporate discount. "I work for a large company. When I was transferred to Nashville, no one I worked with was aware that there was a person at our home office who would send you corporate discounts just for the asking. I use them for everything from motel rooms (up to 50 percent off) to Magic Kingdom Club Cards for discounts to Disneyland. If you work for a large company, even if you have a menial job, be aware that your corporate office may have discounts or freebies that can be yours for the asking."

Gwen Young said her husband Charles is the "cheapest of the cheap." She calls him "Mr. Cheap" and provided this "classic example of his ingenuity and cheapness" in furnishing their renovated attic: "We found two Colonial poster twin beds at a flea market and were able to procure them for $25 each. Then we looked at new mattresses and decided we could not afford them. We had a king-sized mattress made of heavy thick foam rubber, which we had been using up there. He took a chain saw and, you guessed it, split it in two pieces. Foam debris was everywhere, but he was able to dissect that king mattress, making two twins. With duct tape, he secured the ragged edges of both, and we bought mattress pads that entirely covered the chain saw massacre. The latest ingenious thing he did was the installation of bi-fold closet doors as shutters for the exterior of our house. We found these at a garage sale for $25."

Joyce Hughey suggested consulting the newspaper classified ads and responding to requests for models or hair models by companies that are putting on shows in area hotels. She did and had her hair cut, permed, and styled; received a makeover; and got a free lunch, a free goodie bag, and a cash payment of $50, to boot.

Kay Crowder said she uses an insulated six-pack cooler bag as a CD carrier. "It holds fifteen to twenty CDs, is easy to carry, and protects the CDs. And the best is that everybody has two or three they have received as giveaways, compared to the $10 and up that CD carriers cost."

Ken Lass is promoting the "principle of having less. In our acquisitive society, we're geared toward having more stuff. I'm increasingly working toward owning less and thus having fewer clothes to wash, less food to throw away from the rear of the fridge, and fewer repairs to make for this or that machine. I'm no ascetic or hermit, but I just find that my quality of life has improved as the quantity of objects has lessened and the bonus is saving."

Lynn Perry uses leftover wallpaper to line drawers and shelves and as wrapping paper for gifts.

Make your own insulated carry-all that will hold either hot or cold items and is ideal for picnics. "Wrap a popcorn can with newspaper. Use a whole paper so that you can go around the can many times and be sure to wrap the bottom. You can wrap the top separately or wrap it shut and then cut the paper away. Next slip the can into a tripled tall garbage bag and you have an insulated container that will keep ice-cold beverages cold for hours. You can also keep hot things hot. The cans are worth buying with the popcorn. Just save it for later use." —Mary McEwen

Margarette Brown says not to underestimate the power and versatility of panty hose. She uses them not only to tie plants, but to tie garbage bags and even as part of an emergency kit in her trunk. "One man said he used one for a broken fan belt until he could get a few miles to a service station!"

Mary Ann Lentz, a teacher, says she made a drawer divider out of the black plastic flat that her husband had brought home bedding plants in.

"I scrubbed it out and, lo, a desk drawer organizer. It keeps pens, pins, and other supplies and is also the right size for computer disks."

Mitzi Shewmake has a cool idea for swimming free. "That's right, with little more than just asking, most private swim clubs will give your family a free day or even a week pass to try out their facilities. With a little luck and a little chutzpah, your family can be swimming all summer."

Nancy Gamble has a creative use for leftover toilet paper rolls. "I use them to keep my cords from getting tangled up. I just fold up my cords and flip them up in there. I use them on my curling irons, my iron, my electric skillet, etc."

Pat Harper uses a piece of dry spaghetti in place of those long fireplace matches to light a fire or a pilot light.

Vikki Harris says when she wore out her footies, she realized that they would make good dusters by just putting them on her hands and dusting away.

"Need some touch-up paint, but the stuff in the can is lumpy and separated? Fit part of the leg of an old panty hose over the top of a cut-off milk jug. Pour the paint into the panty hose and squeeze it through into the milk jug." —*Carole Kenner*

Billy Fiveash of Hendersonville, Tennessee, was the recipient of the first annual cheapest of the cheap "Highpockets" award. Included in his slew of tips for around the house are some serious ones and some that are very tongue-in-cheek:

- Put up a clothesline to dry clothes, and save electricity.
- Send the kids to a Third World country where they can be fed, clothed, and educated for $12 a month.
- Visit a friend on Sunday and read his newspaper.
- Make friends with people who have kids a year or so older than yours. That way you can get their outgrown clothes, hopefully free.
- In winter, keep the house cooler and put on more clothes when inside.
- Be sure to visit friends and kinfolk when their garden is in. Get free tomatoes, beans, corn, etc.
- Learn to identify and find wild plants that can be eaten. Free.
- Learn to make your own beer and wine. A big, big savings.
- In the rare event a cheap person must rent a carpet shampooer, try to find a friend who needs one also, and both use it and split the rental fee.
- In summer, use electric fans to keep cool as long as possible without turning on the air conditioning, to save electricity.
- Use little or no heat in the bedrooms. Use electric blankets or snuggle to keep warm.

Artist Velma Flatt watches for sales on small pictures already framed, takes the commercial pictures out, and puts her originals in. "They look really good, and I save quite a bit by not having them framed at an art and frame store."

"An easy and safe way to kill bugs is to spray hair spray on them. It makes their legs stick together and then you can pick them up and throw them away." —*Julie Smothers*

"Buy a pound of rice (50¢), pour the rice into a stray sock, shift the rice to lie loosely, cut off the excess, and sew up the open edge. This makes a cheap, comfortable computer wrist rest, which would cost $3.99 or more at stores." —*Carmel Redmon*

"I fill gallon jugs with water and freeze them. Then when we need ice for a camp-out or homemade ice cream, there it is in the freezer." —*Mary Nell Paris*

"I make coasters out of foam plates. You can decorate them any way you want." —*Ella Crowston*

"I use plastic grocery bags as gloves for picking up grass clippings or other messy items, and then just throw them away with the messy job." —*Lorrie Sawyer*

"Chew only a half piece of gum." —*Bill Turner*

"Just remember, rich doesn't necessarily mean you have mucho buckaroos. You can still be rich, if you know how to handle life. It's not what you have, it's how you spend it." —*the Clements family*

"My cheap idea is to save baby food jars and attach them underneath cabinets, for storage of small items. Place a screw through the center of the baby food lid underneath the cabinet. The jar can be screwed on and off the lid." —*Addie Gilliam*

"My way to be Ms. Cheap is to call the toll-free numbers on products. I just got $20 from Signature Goods as I bought some ground sirloin and it was kind of dark in the middle. Still good, but I wanted to know why it was a different color. I also got more than my money back from Tyson because the giblets were missing. I got free mayonnaise from Hellmann's because I didn't like the slaw dressing. It pays to call the toll-free numbers." —*Rita Spradling*

"We hike with the Tennessee Trails group, so we freeze our drinking water in recycled soft drink bottles. We each place two of the frozen bottles with a sandwich in between (the ice keeps the food from spoiling) in a heavy-duty cereal bag and put the bag in our backpacks. It keeps our packs and our backs from getting damp and messy. It is also great to drink the cold, thawed bottled water on a hot day." —*Sue Eldridge*

"I keep my water heater off most of the time. I turn it on for about fifteen minutes for a shower and save $20 to $30 a month." —*Liz Schneider*

Charlie Dunaway uses his empty Tic Tac containers for salt and pepper shakers for his lunch box.

"Check curbside for tossed furniture that can be touched up, used, or sold." —*Bill Turner*

Esther Hudson gets ideas from catalogs and copies them, everything from dickeys (which she makes from old blouses) to a jigsaw puzzle mat to magazine files, which she makes out of empty detergent boxes.

Michele Chaffin's "proudest cheap moment" was winning eight *Anastasia on Ice* tickets in a radio contest. "I sold four tickets to a friend for $20. I parked at my brother-in-law's place of employment (two blocks from the arena)—free parking. I saw the show, got a little exercise, and came out with $20!"

Paul Nance is too cheap to eat lunch out every day, yet too lazy to make it every morning. So he buys a loaf of bread and luncheon meat. "Here's the good part. To keep my bread from going bad before I can use the whole loaf, after taking out two pieces each day, I quickly close the bag and suck the air out completely. The tricky part is not sucking too hard (that smushes the bread), and not being seen."

"When shopping for towels and washcloths, I was pleased to see large bath towels for $4.99. The washcloths were $2.99 or $3.99 each. I bought one extra bath towel and no washcloths. I cut the extra towel into eight eleven-by-eleven-inch squares. Using a heavy-duty needle and heavy-duty thread, I zigzagged all four edges. Voilà!" —*Dee Weisbarth*

Resourceful Alice Huang made jump ropes out of used-up pens and plastic tubes and free rubber bands from vegetables and newspapers. The pens are the handles and the looped-together rubber bands are the rope. "It's colorful and works well."

"Buy designer eyeglass frames for $4 to $6 at a discount store. Bring them to an optician (Wal-Mart, etc.) with your lens prescription. The result is affordable prescription sunglasses!" —*Mary Burney*

"To keep luggage smelling fresh, put a fabric softener sheet in it when not in use." —*Lynn Yuchnitz*

"To make a great desk organizer, use six or seven Pringle cans. Cover each with pretty contact paper and group them on an inexpensive turntable. It's great for pencils, pens, scissors, rulers, and so on." —*Corrine Fuson*

"My idea about saving money is don't spend what you don't have." —*Linda Coney*

"Save those plastic onion bags. Tip 1: They're perfect for hanging bird seed balls made from lard and birdseed. Tip 2: Roll them up or tie them together to use as pot scrubbers or for getting hard spilled spots off your floors." —*Virginia Grove*

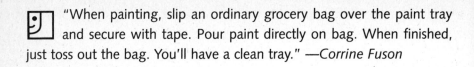 "When painting, slip an ordinary grocery bag over the paint tray and secure with tape. Pour paint directly on bag. When finished, just toss out the bag. You'll have a clean tray." —*Corrine Fuson*

"Don't tell anyone you have money, so they can't ask for it." —*Sandra Brazerol*

"I bought an old beat-up secretary, repainted it, and bored a small hole in the back for the wires to my computer. I now have a very attractive work station that cost $8, and it is different from any computer desk I have seen." —*Daphne Lyons*

"In our area, neighborhood, circle of friends and family, there are all sizes and shapes of men, women, and children. What we do is rotate clothes, shoes, and whatever we have that is usable—even cookware and dishes—and let someone else have them. In this way, we have new and different stuff all the time—bedspreads, curtains, throw rugs, the list never ends. When everyone is finished with an item, it is donated to Goodwill." —*Marie Herndon*

"Make a mixture of alcohol and water and put it in a spray bottle. Use this with paper towels for handy wipes." —*Mary McEwen*

"While on vacation, instead of buying a bag of ice at a minimarket, my sister and I asked how much a cup of ice cost. We were told 15¢. We asked if we could refill our cup free and were told yes, so we just kept refilling the cup and putting the ice into our cooler until it was full, and all it cost us was 15¢." —*Teena Thompson*

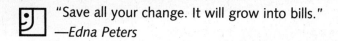 "Save all your change. It will grow into bills."
—*Edna Peters*

"To remove snow and ice from porches and sidewalks, use baking soda." —*JoAnn Bazzell*

"Use Bounce dryer sheets to repel mice and rats. They do not like the smell." —*Donna Michelle Copas*

"Use mesh bags like fruit comes in to make bird feeders. Fill with medium- to large-sized birdseed. Tie the end and hang from a bird feed holder or a nail. For smaller seed, double the bag. The birds hang off the side and love these feeders." —*Sheilia Bleam*

Caroline Collins says to open large envelopes very carefully and reuse as filing folders in your filing cabinet.

"Don't throw away those one-sided computer papers. Make another pile of paper to run for another one-sided job or save and donate for scrap paper." —*Lottie Robey*

"Repairs can be made to nicks and spots in anything that has gold trim, such as a picture frame, by applying gold leaf, either plain or

antique. Small bottles of gold leaf can be purchased in hardware stores."
—*Carmen Pearson*

"When the sprayer won't let you use the remainder of the liquid in your container, put a straw over the stem." —*Connie Wynn*

"Make your own fly paper by spreading honey on yellow paper. Then fill a sprayer with soapy water and spray the trapped flies with it." —*Bruce Hawkins*

"Many candles seem to burn down through the middle and leave a lot of wax around the sides. I hated throwing away all of that scrap, so I chipped the wax into a potpourri pot. Smells wonderful! It can be used day after day and won't evaporate like potpourri." —*Corrine Fuson*

Lynn Yuchnitz says she carries a three-inch pad in her purse with a list of things she would like to replace in her home. "This is not a list of items I must have but of items I'd like to replace when found on sale or clearance," she says. For example, she lists mini-blinds, with a note about the size, length, and room, and an area rug with size and desired colors.

10

Being Cheap to Be Generous

Some folks think being cheap means being stingy, greedy, unethical, or so tight that you can't (or won't) give anything away. However, I'm not promoting that kind of cheapness. I believe you can and should be cheap in order to be generous. What it all boils down to is getting the most for my money, not being wasteful, and being a good steward of my money. I believe my kind of cheap is a positive kind, a cheapness you can be proud of!

Many of you have shown me ways to be cheap in order to be generous—ways you save money and stretch your dollars for good causes. I want to share these "cheap but generous" ideas with you.

Tips: Being Generous

Ardyce House says she gets as many angels as possible off the Salvation Army Angel Tree by buying a year ahead. "January through

April, or later, I buy girls' clothes, jewelry, accessories, toys, games for a girl aged fourteen. I pick the angels for this age and right now have an ample supply for four to six girls, cheap. If I didn't do this, I could only get one or two angels. All these items are new. I get much joy and satisfaction from doing this."

"During the year, we like to buy office items that are free with rebates at Office Max, CompUSA, and other stores, and then pass them on to agencies or people who need them. We have donated some to our church auction to help raise money for missions, and now we will pass some on to the Boys & Girls Club. Donating items you already have and aren't using won't cost you anything, except the time and gas you use delivering them." —Lynda Duncan

"Pick nonperishable items from the coupons in the Sunday paper. Then go to any store that doubles the value of coupons. You can use your coupons to make up several gift baskets (food, etc.) for others. I do this for my mother, who doesn't like to shop, and for housewarming gifts. I put the stuff in a laundry basket or any other colorful container. This is an inexpensive gift, and is especially appreciated by friends who are unemployed." —Joyce Stults

Esther Hudson was walking in her neighborhood and noticed garbage cans loaded with dolls (china dolls, Barbies) and other toys. She went to the door to ask if she could have them, but no one was home. She and her daughter dashed home, got bags, and returned to fill them with the "trash." They then sent the dolls and toys to a missionary friend in the Philippines for children there.

Lynn Yuchnitz says she "picks up new toys on clearance or at garage sales during the year to donate at Christmas to needy kids."

"Save the unused shampoo, soap, body lotion, and shower caps from hotel and motel rooms, and then take them to homeless shelters when you get home." —*Dot Hodges*

"Often when grocery shopping, we find we can get free or nearly free items we don't need or don't really like or probably won't use. What to do? Get all the free and super-cheap nonperishable items as possible. Fill sacks with the extras and give to a food bank." —*Diane Floyd*

"Keep a box or strong paper bag handy and when you shop, drop an item in it every so often for places like the food bank. You won't miss these items, and you'll have a wonderful feeling for doing this." —*Evelyn Hooper*

Diane Cull gets free hair color and makeup through coupons and rebating, then gives them to her local senior citizens center.

Peggy Carpenter is always looking for deals for her Seroptimist Club's service projects. She recently spotted a 79¢-off coupon in a Kroger flyer for Suave shampoo and hair products and noticed that Kroger had the items on sale for 79¢, making them essentially free. She called her fellow Seroptimists, and they scrounged enough coupons to get 285 bottles of the hair products free, then donated them to Ronald McDonald House, the Domestic Violence Shelter, and Mercy Ministries.

Linda Solina loaded up on coats for children at the Goodwill Salvage Store, where they sell clothes by the pound. "I got a whole big bag of great coats for about $5." She took the coats to DryClean USA to be cleaned free, then donated them to Coats for Kids.

Ruth Ann Harnisch says to check out the Website www.thehunger-site.com and click the box that reads "donate free food." For every click, the sponsors give a certain amount of food to the United Nations World Food program in return for advertising links. "You can click only once a day, but if everybody did it once a day, wow!" They've already given almost five million pounds of food.

"Several years ago, when my children were poor teenagers, I suggested that instead of buying gifts for their father and me for Christmas, they donate one day of their time to a charitable organization in our name. They all did, and it has continued to be a tradition in our family. One daughter donates a day to visiting in the VA Hospital, my son spends one day a year serving meals at the mission, and one daughter works with the angel tree program. Now that my children are grown and can afford expensive gifts, they continue to do this for me and as a way of giving back to the community." —*Cynthia Atkins*

"I collect soda cans in big garbage bags. I take them to my church on Wednesday night when the homeless people come in to eat and sleep. I wanted to share the aluminum cans with all the people, so I let each person take home some cans as they leave in the morning. This is an easy way to give to others, and it's good for my church, too." —*Brendan Kiefer*

"We don't throw away aluminum cans. We save them up and take them to the Lions Club Aluminum Can Recycling Trailer, where the club helps buy eyeglasses for local children and adults who otherwise couldn't afford to buy them." —*Walter Bowen Sr.*

"My senior citizen club has a fundraiser that anyone can do—recycling greeting cards. They cut out the front picture and message and the message inside, glue them to a new card (white or cream), outline the glued-on part with a marking pen in a coordinating color, and supply new envelopes. They sell for 25¢. Do it yourself for the cost of plain cards and envelopes." —*Shirley Hereth*

Rachel Sumner advises, "Apartment dwellers should always be on the lookout at the dumpsters around the end of the month. I am appalled at the good clothes people throw away." She and her husband found nine huge garbage bags full of designer clothes, which they donated to Goodwill.

Dianne Gregory picks up change from the drive-through window at local restaurants and drops it in the Ronald McDonald House collection box.

"My husband and I and sometimes our whole office attend many trade shows where promotional items are given away. One of the items we pick up religiously is pencils, sometimes asking for an extra one or two. At the end of the show, we gather all the pencils and donate them to the local elementary school. You can also collect door prizes and other giveaways and donate them to a school fundraiser. I also send goodie bags to the group home where my brother lives, and it's a thrill for the residents to open packages and see the new pens, pencils, drink holders, etc." —*Lesly Hart-Kelly*

"Most product rebates are limited to one per household. When I see a great bargain, I buy double and send the cash-back rebate to a friend's address. I like to think they are greatly surprised to find a $5 or more check in their mailbox." —*Darlene Hardin*

Gayle Douglas collects aluminum cans for her church and turns them in for money. "People bring them to my house and put them at the mailbox for me to take."

"Instead of sending flowers when someone dies, I send the family a book of stamps. The receiver will personally call and thank me for such a nice idea." —*Gladys Denning*

"Be a 4-H volunteer leader. The thanks you get from the young people is rewarding. Call your local extension agent in your county for more information." —*Marcella Spence*

"My husband goes to trade shows and gets the ballpoint pens that are given away for advertising. I donate them to the crisis centers. It cuts down on their operating costs." —*Sandra Hackney*

"I collect used fruit baskets and fill them with fruit, candy, or other items to take to the sick and shut-ins." —*Shirley Bell*

"I donate money to charity and get 'forced' exercise by parking in a free lot farther from my office and walking ten minutes twice each day. Now I send my favorite charity a check instead of sending the parking company a check every month." —*Bettie Tiesler*

"I grocery shop for shut-ins and I also clip coupons from the newspaper for them, as well as for myself. They are on a very limited income, and the savings gives them money to spend on other things they need and want." —*Marie Brantley*

"I have contacted companies for free recipe booklets and asked them if they would please send an extra to a friend. They were surprise little gifts that were a great hit!" —*Karen Buckwold*

Lolly Webster says her church has a unique gift idea for a sick or lonely person: "Because we are all on a limited budget, this is a way to show we care and are thinking about someone, without spending a lot of money. We each bring an envelope to our once-a-month breakfast. In the envelope, we put anything that will fit—a handwritten prayer, a get well message, a bookmark, a greeting card, a cheery note, a pin, a magnet, or any little memento. All the filled envelopes are put in a gift bag, and the bag is given to someone who is sick or recovering from surgery or whatever."

If you have too many cassettes, "tape a special radio program on a cassette that you do not use anymore and give it to someone who would enjoy it." —*Mary Nell Paris*

"When I was pregnant and after my children were born, I received lots of free samples of formula and coupons for free formula. Since I didn't use it, I redeemed all the coupons and took the formula to the local food bank. They were delighted to get the donation and I felt great doing it." —*Laurie Smith*

"I order baby items and toys from www.cyberrebate.com, which offers a 100 percent rebate. There is no charge for mailing. Then I am able to give these gifts/prizes to the customers at our Pathways Meetings at NashvilleWorks. Sixteen weeks later, I receive my total reimbursement at no expense to me. The baby items and toys are a wonderful incentive for the women." —*Jeanne Kauss*

Al Frazier says he saves all the ball caps and T-shirts that he gets during the year and gives them to his sister to take to South America on her annual summer trip there as a volunteer worker.

Al Frazier says he saves all the ball caps and T-shirts that he gets during the year and gives them to his sister to take to South America on her annual summer trip there as a volunteer worker.

"My suggestion for saving money while benefiting others is surely not for everyone and probably ought not be pursued for purely money-saving reasons. Donating one's body for medical research saves the cost of burial. The school or wherever will cremate the remains and inter them when they are through with the body, which may take two to four years." —*Susan Greer*

"I donate blood for the Red Cross at my company's donation drive. Not only is one unit helpful for six lives, but my company has drawings and gives vacation hours, discount meal tickets, and T-shirts to donors." —*Marie Gregory*

"Do volunteer work. It keeps you from being somewhere else spending money and often provides you with contacts that will save you money somewhere along the line." —*Donna Montgomery*

"Use the shoe shine cloth/sponge from your hotel stay and a packet of dry yeast as a basis for your mailing to a special ailing friend or neighbor, with this greeting: 'Hope you'll soon be able to rise and shine.' The recipient will feel better right away, and you'll save about three quarters of the cost of an average-priced greeting card." —*Vivian Reynolds*

"Since my husband and I both play tennis, we have an excess of tennis balls. Just recently we found that people using walkers have a real need for tennis balls to use as safety cups." —*Mary Lou Gallagher*

"I purchase cheap vases at yard sales and flea markets all year long and so have plenty available when my flower garden and rose garden are in bloom. That way it is easy to give flowers away to friends and people just needing something to brighten their day." —*June Ross*

"My way of being generous but cheap revolves around the newspaper. For years, I have saved my papers for a neighbor down the street. Then I realized that my next-door neighbors would also enjoy reading them, as they do not subscribe. So I drop yesterday's paper at their door on the way to get today's paper, and they save them for the neighbor down the street. So many times, if we would take the time, we could find that we each have something to offer a neighbor or friend." —*Nellie Daugherty*

"When I go through the U-Scan at Kroger, I always check the trash cans next to each position for receipts that other people have thrown away. I always get them out and put them in our school's collection box. The school gets a percentage of every dollar spent so my 'fishing' helps the school make money." —*Andrea Hyssong*

"Throughout the year, I watch for great sales on popular toys— Barbies, Matchbox cars, games, etc.—and then at Christmastime I donate them to Toys for Tots. Usually I have two bags. My three- and four-year-olds help pick out some of the items, and it teaches them about sharing, too." —*Kim Helper*

Karen Hawkins says her church does mission work with Native Americans in South Dakota. "Each year the schools are desperate for school supplies, so last year, as the stores were having their sales on back-to-school supplies, I bought the maximum at each store, sometimes getting notebook paper for 10¢, pens for 5¢, and so on. When the mission team goes on its trip, I send the supplies."

"At garage sales, I often offer to come back and pick up unbought baby items for the Crisis Pregnancy Center, clothing and household items for Appalachian missions, or Bibles for the ministry I work for overseas. Frequently people tell me to go ahead and take them. Hence, last weekend I picked up a VCR for the Crisis Pregnancy Center and a set of encyclopedias and a Bible for a Bible school in Africa. Sometimes all it takes is your time and a little storage space until someone can pick up the items."
—*Karen Hawkins*

"Save aluminum pie pans; clean and fill by doubling a recipe. Freeze and take to a neighbor, shut-in, or busy mother." —*Carmel Redmon*

Linda Spitzer says she and her children look out for clearance flowers and then repot them and take them to seniors to brighten their day. "We know how the sweet faces of these seniors will light up when Matthew and Hannah bless them with a surprise visit and gift. I love to see my children's faces as they delight in bringing joy to others. It is a good thing that we can do so much with so little."

"My aunt was at Bordeaux Hospital for fifteen years. I would visit every Sunday. Before leaving, I would visit each room on her ward and ask if they needed anything. Sometimes they would request small items—a radio, a clock, a case for their eyeglasses, a new book. The next Saturday, I would go on my cheap expedition to garage sales and look for the requested items. I usually found what I was looking for, and if I told the seller it was for a nursing home, I would get a good deal or sometimes even get the item free. So keep someone in mind when you are on your quest for bargains." —*Nancy Burton*

"Never turn down anything free. If you can't use it, you probably know someone who can." —*Linda Rivers*

"Throughout the year I look for and buy products that can be used by our local women's shelter and are offered as 'freebates' at the store. I have to pay only the tax on the product by using the store coupon or special offer. Then at Christmastime, I can donate these items. Last year I was able to donate almost $200 in products this way with my cost being only $14 for the tax paid, plus a small amount for postage." — *Eleanor Hausa-Josephs*

11

Tips That Are Waaaaay Out There

When I first started my "Ms. Cheap" column in the spring of 1994, I thought I was cheap. My husband thought I was cheap, our daughters thought I was cheap, and most of my friends thought I was cheap. But I am here to tell you that there are a lot of people out there who are cheaper than I am.

I had a man tell me that he peels his bananas before he checks out at the grocery store so that they weigh less.

Another man wrote the *Tightwad Gazette*, bragging about the fact that he lived on eight rolls of toilet paper a year. Just read his letter if you want down-and-out cheap: "I have been a natural for tightwaddery since birth (1932). I can remember with horror that when I was about twelve my seven-year-old sister would spin the toilet paper roll with reckless abandon until she had at least two yards all over the place just to take care of a little. . . . I resolved to use but two squares myself and ever since have been just as frugal. I can make do on eight rolls of toilet paper per year. That includes guests, wiping off eyeglasses, and occasionally blowing my nose."

Can you believe that? There are a lot of these thoroughly cheap people. There was a man who told me that he digs into the couches when he visits friends and neighbors in hopes that the previous occupant may have lost some change.

I knew I had arrived as Ms. Cheap when I got a call with what I considered a thoroughly disgusting suggestion. The caller said that too many people waste Q-tips. "It seems to me that after you use them to clean your ears, you could save them to clean the car's air conditioner vents. They already have the dust catcher on them." Ugh!

> One of the best ways to measure people is to watch the way they behave when something free is offered.
>
> —Ann Landers

I had a lady suggest that you "empty the contents of your baby's diaper on your shrubs and use it as fertilizer." A P.S. scribbled at the bottom advised, "only do this to the outside plants." I am not making this up.

I had a lady tell me that she used duct tape to hold her false teeth in place. I'm serious. This is what she wrote: "My experience with duct tape: When eating corn on the cob, I broke three front teeth on the upper partial. I refuse to go anyplace without my teeth. Knowing not to use Super Glue and having to go to the grocery store, I did not know what to do. Then this bright idea came to me: Use a very small piece of duct tape to hold these teeth in. It worked until I finished shopping and got home. The taste was not pleasant, but I did not mind. My dentist could not believe what I had done, but the tape did no damage to the partial."

These are true stories. I had a woman call and tell me that she gathers up the hair that collects in her tub and mushes it together and uses it as an abrasive pad to clean her tub. I had a fellow worker tell me that she bought baby shoes for her baby, put them on the baby for the photos in the studio, and then returned the shoes to the store. I got a contest entry suggesting that you "buy a really cute outfit that you will never wear twice, leave the tags on it, wear it, and take it back the next day for a refund." Another contest entrant said that if you want to do the same thing with shoes, just cover the bottoms with clear wide tape to keep them from getting dirty, wear them, remove the tape, and take them back. Another entry was "place used toothpicks in hot soapy water, rinse, pour mouthwash over them, and reuse." How about this one: "You can reuse pregnancy tests as long as the result is negative."

> Only people who like dog food don't save for retirement.
> —Dave Ramsey, author of *Financial Peace*

Some of the ideas were so bizarre I could never print them, but this entry that Eleanor Barrett of Nashville sent in as a joke is so funny that I just have to share it. Barrett says she wrote this for fun: "I was kidding and thought you might get a laugh." I did. I laughed out loud! You can tell that Barrett had a good time coming up with these wacko cheaper-than-cheap ideas. I hope you will enjoy reading them too. Please don't take them too seriously. It is a *joke!* Here are Eleanor's ideas:

- Don't throw away your bacon grease. It makes good night cream. If your husband doesn't cuddle up, your dog is sure to.
- Iron damp paper towels and reuse.
- Line the baby's playpen with an old shower curtain liner. Let him play nude. The air will feel good on his body, and you can hose down the baby and the playpen and save several diapers a day.
- Wear your underpants two days. The first day, wear the regular way, and the second day, turn them inside out. This will save on soap, water, and wear and tear on the underwear. (Believe it or not, this was a serious entry in a previous contest.)
- Don't flush when you only urinate. Save that water for important stuff.
- Save up your dirty clothes until it rains. Then put on as many clothes as you can, grab a cake of soap you lifted from that last motel, and have a blast singing in the rain.
- Save all that junk mail and use it as toilet paper.
- Carry big, almost-empty purses. Visit the ladies' room, and carry home one of their spare rolls of toilet paper.
- Crash wedding receptions for a free evening out. Take a large empty box wrapped with bridal paper. Add a lovely bow, congratulate the bride and groom, eat and drink all you can, and dance the night away.
- Make your own Q-tips. Take old fashioned stick matches. Use cotton wisely saved from aspirin bottles, and wrap a thin layer of cotton around the top. When you've used it, you can strike the match and burn all that yucky stuff you put on it.

- Free baby-sitting is plentiful in church nurseries. Drop Junior off, and go merrily on your way for a few hours. If you're late getting back and the nursery attendants are a little testy, have excuses ready that match the particular church. For example, "I was slain in the spirit and just came out of it" (Pentecostal); "The confessional door got stuck and I just got out" (Catholic); "I was helping count the collection for Lottie Moon" (Baptist); "I was collecting used communion cups" (Church of Christ); "The pastor didn't have enough faith and the snake bit him and I was sucking out the venom" (snake handlers).

Thank you so much, Eleanor, for sharing this funny cheapo stuff.

Anyway, I am often amused and flabbergasted by some of the tips that come my way and thought you might enjoy them, too. Again, I must tell you I am not suggesting that you do these things, and again, I promise you that I do not do any of these things.

This is my list of ideas that fall into the category of "maybe life is too short to be this cheap!"

Tips: Waaaaay Out There

"When using a tissue to blot lipstick or even just lightly blow your nose, drop into a container and use later as toilet paper."

"I always bought the widest sheets available. When the center became weak and worn, I tore them down the center and sewed the strong unused sides together, making a like-new sheet. When my son went to Harvard, that is what I packed for him to carry. This caused a near riot among his well-to-do roommates. They never saw a sheet with a seam down the middle. They already believed that only barefoot illiterates came from the South."

One lady says to toast one slice of bread and "holding it vertically, slice downward. You have two pieces of toast for a sandwich made from one piece of bread." Now that is thin sliced!

This idea was poohpoohed by the IRS, which says not to do it: "Buy free with double coupons even those groceries and sundries that your family doesn't use, and donate them to appropriate not-for-profit organizations (food banks, shelters) at retail value for a federal tax deduction. Depending on your tax bracket, you may receive a third of the value of your donations in tax saved with no cash outlay. Benefits: (1) You get to shop and spend no money. (2) You save on your taxes and have more money in your pocket. (3) You get a good feeling." (I actually thought this one was pretty good until I called the IRS to check it out.)

A man sent in a tip suggesting do-it-yourself burials. He enclosed an article from Farm Show magazine that says that in all but seven states you can take care of all of the funeral arrangements yourself without a funeral director. "If you would rather be buried in a pine box out on the back forty than go through all the rigmarole and expense of a big funeral, you just might want to contact the Rev. Forrest Hayes of Middlebury,

Indiana. He publishes a series of do-it-yourself manuals to conduct your own funeral service without getting a funeral director involved." Hayes suggests that "you can bury the body on your own property in many states." For more information, write Farm Show Followup, Burial, P.O. Box 1402, Middlebury, IN 46540.

"After your guests have finished their tea or lemonade, collect the ice, wash it off, and return it to the ice bin."

"Several years ago on a budget tour of Europe, we were staying at a small hotel in Paris where the bathroom was down the hall. To take a bath, you had to pay the hotel $1.00 for water and $.25 for an extra bath towel. My traveling friend asked me to leave the water in the tub for her bath, which I did, and then a stranger asked her to leave the water for another bath. Do I have a cheap friend or what?" (This must have been a long time ago!)

> Spending less is better than earning more.
>
> —Paul A. Wilson, author of *Real Men Use Coupons*

"For a satisfying cheap cup of tomato soup in a restaurant, order a cup of hot tea with lemon and a tea bag on the side. Fill the cup half full with hot water, add tomato ketchup until the cup is three-quarters full, add a pinch of salt and pepper, stir well. Squeeze a bit of lemon into the cup and stir again. Drink and enjoy. Slip the tea bag into your purse and take it home to be used later. If you are bold enough, ask for a pack of crackers."

"Each day before leaving the office at 4:30, I make it a point to go to the rest room for one last time. This way, I don't have to flush my toilet so much at home, thus helping my water bill and also saving toilet tissue. At home, I save water by flushing the toilet every other time. Water is not cheap, you know, but I am."

"To use the calendar for next year, you simply change the days of the week across the top and you are ready to use again. It's already marked with important dates, birthdays, anniversaries, etc. You save $10 a year for a calendar and maybe two hours of time used to purchase and mark appropriately. Over a lifetime of 75 years, that is $750 and 150 hours. Boy, do I know how to spend that savings."

"I buy Vanity Fair paper napkins for special occasions and then cut them in half for everyday family dinners."

"I use wigs and buy one only occasionally. It is so much cheaper than having my hair done every week, and they are always ready to go."

"I think the very cheapest thing I do to save money concerns my underwear. I, like most other men, hate to get rid of my old Fruit of the Looms. So instead of tossing them, I recycle the waistband and use it for a sweatband for my head. Don't laugh until you have tried it. It really works well, especially if you leave enough of the other material of the shorts to wrap around the elastic waistband to make it more absorbent."

"Next time you're smearing roll-on deodorant in that ugly armpit of yours, imagine the little rolly ball removed from its plastic socket, dried off, and hung on your Christmas tree via a bent paper clip."

Look at this efficient recipe for "beautiful complexion with breakfast": "After breaking eggs for your family's breakfast, run your fingers inside the shells for the remaining egg whites and cover your face with them. Let it dry while preparing breakfast, then rinse off and pat dry for a radiant complexion. Then bake the shells in the oven to dry them, and place them in the blender to make a powdered bone meal, which is a good plant fertilizer. In this way, every part of the egg is used completely."

"Steal other people's recycling from the curb and redeem it for cash at the recycling center. Rinse and reuse dental floss. Who wants to spend $5 to $10 each year on a pumpkin at Halloween? Freeze your jack-o'-lantern from year to year. If you have a big freezer and a small tree, do the same with your Christmas tree."

"Now that stems have come back to watches, I have discovered that if you pull it out to set the time, it also stops the watch. I can pull the stem before I go to bed and I give my battery extra life. Cheap, huh?"

"My husband is so cheap that he saves all of the extra fast food ketchup packets and when he collects a few, he squeezes them into the ketchup bottle. You would be surprised at how long a bottle of ketchup lasts in our house." —"Mr. Cheap's Wife"

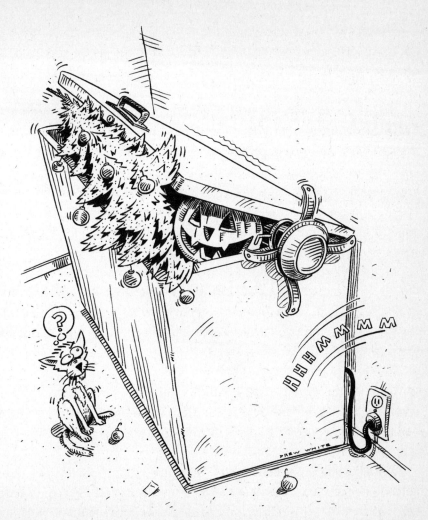

Freeze your jack-o'-lantern and Christmas tree from year-to-year.

One lady buys unused, still-in-the-box items at yard sales and returns them to stores. "I spent $2.50 for five things, and I was able to take them back and get a credit for $35."

"Save the empty cardboard roll that toilet tissue comes in. Purchase two-ply toilet tissue and roll one ply to the empty carton you have saved. You will have two rolls of toilet tissue."

> The easiest way to make money is to trim expenses.
> —Alan Greenberg, CEO of Bear Stearns

"My friend and I will go to a buffet, and she will order the buffet. I will order only a drink. I then will eat off her plate, and we will split the bill."

One of my coworkers has family living nine hours away, so at the beginning of each trip, his first stop is McDonald's for a regular-sized coffee to go. Then he stops at other McDonald's all along the way for his 'free refill.' This same paper cup can also be used on the return trip."

"At some movie theaters you can get a free refill on a large popcorn by bringing the original bag back to the concession stand. The cost of a large popcorn is usually about $4.50. Keep the bag and take it back the next time you go and save."

This is a recipe for "Tennessee shrimp." The ingredients are a white turnip, batter of your choice, oil for frying, and shrimp sauce. "Peel the turnip and slice as for french fries. Batter and deep fry and serve with sauce. Tastes like shrimp if you don't know the difference."

"When we invite a couple over for dinner, my wife and I serve hot tea. We pour four cups of hot water and use one tea bag. Of course, we let the company dunk first."

"Often the department stores will offer a nice gift if you spend $25 at the fragrance counter. Buy the fragrance of your choice and get the free gift, which you can give away at Christmas or as a birthday gift. And if you wait a few weeks, you can return the fragrance for credit and you still have the free gift. Cheap, yes, but isn't that what we are talking about?"

"Save the suckers and hard candy you get when you go to the bank or restaurants. On October 31, you guessed it, give it to the trick-or-treaters. Make sure the candy is securely wrapped."

About flushing—"if it's yellow, let it mellow, if it's brown, flush it down!"

"Buy something very nice like an antique collectible that you would like to have for yourself and give it to a very old relative or loved one. Make sure you put your name on the bottom of the gift in permanent ink, like 'to my favorite great aunt whom I love deeply.' When this loved one passes on, you'll get your gift back. Plus you have a better shot at being in the will."

12

Ethics Quiz: How Cheap Is Too Cheap?

Years ago, when I first started writing my "Ms. Cheap" column, I got in big trouble with readers when I suggested taking food and drink into movie theaters to enjoy during movies. Several readers said it was clearly against the rules and that I was sending a mixed message to my children. At that time I developed an ethics survey patterned after one I had seen in the now-defunct *Tightwad Gazette*. I decided they were right—that some cheap strategies were over the edge—and I amended my ways (pretty much).

Well, I hit a nerve again in a later column where I mentioned that I took a "smidgen" of cilantro off of a salsa bar and took it home to put in a party dip. I justified my action by saying I could just as easily have put the cilantro on my salad and eaten it at the restaurant, but instead, deferred my consumption. I got several calls telling me that my cilantro heist was beyond the bounds of ethical cheapness and that I should *not* have taken it.

So I revised the earlier ethics survey and ran it again. What follows is a combination of the two surveys that is designed to elicit your feelings on what is ethical and not ethical within the world of cheapdom. Each and every question posed in the survey was included as a result of readers writing or calling me to say that they did these things (or similar things) or knew someone who did. I want to be sure that you know that I am *not* trying to get you to do unethical things, but rather to define for yourself where the lines are.

My hope is for the survey to be provocative, for it to get you talking and thinking about what is ethical and what is not and where you draw the line. I hope that parents will survey their children, and children their parents, and that those fine lines between right and wrong will become more clear. Cheapness will grow a little less hazy as a result.

The possible answers are:
A. Yes, it is ethical.
B. Yes, it is ethical, but I wouldn't do it.
C. No, it is not ethical.
D. No, it is not ethical, but I would do it anyway.

Here goes the survey. Circle the best answer. Is it ethical to:

1. Take a smidgen of cilantro home from a salsa bar instead of putting it on your salad in the restaurant?
   A B C D
2. Take all the unused soap, shampoo, stationery, pens, note pads, etc., from the hotel/motel where you are staying?
   A B C D

3. Take home a few packets of artificial sweetener when you go to a restaurant?

   A B C D

4. Regift, that is, give gifts that you have received and either don't like or won't use?

   A B C D

5. Shop at a thrift store if you have an average or above-average income? (The possible objection would be that you would be buying items less fortunate people need.)

   A B C D

6. Use a coupon at the grocery, knowing it has expired or does not really match the item you are buying?

   A B C D

7. Reuse a postage stamp from a letter that has been delivered but not canceled?

   A B C D

8. Return a ten-year-old coat to L. L. Bean to take advantage of the company's unconditional guarantee?

   A B C D

9. Secretly switch your spouse's favorite expensive name brand with a store brand to see if he or she notices the difference?

   A B C D

10. Take your own snacks into the movie theater, ignoring the signs saying no outside food is allowed?

    A B C D

11. Take an apple or banana from your hotel's free breakfast bar for a later snack?

    A B C D

12. Buy a fragrance to get the free gift, then return the fragrance to the store for credit and keep the free gift?

    A B C D

13. During a long car trip, stop at McDonald's for a coffee to go, then keep refilling the cup with free coffee from other McDonald's along the way?

    A B C D

14. Go to a buffet with a friend and share one buffet meal?

    A B C D

15. Get the newspaper out of the recycle bin instead of buying one?

    A B C D

16. Tear out the advertisements with the scents from the magazines at the doctor's office?

    A B C D

17. Save the extra ketchup packets that come with a fast food meal and squeeze them into your ketchup bottle at home?

    A B C D

18. Accept companies' free offers (such as dinner or an overnight resort stay), even though you know you aren't going to buy anything?

    A B C D

19. Use senior coupons at the grocery even if you aren't a senior?

    A B C D

20. Get two meals for one by ordering an entree that includes soup and

salad bar, pigging out at the salad bar, and then taking the entree home for your next meal?

A B C D

21. Get a free refill on a large popcorn at the movie theater by keeping the bag and taking it back to the concession stand the next time you go to the theater?

A B C D

22. After hospital stays, take home the hygiene items, including small bars of soap, denture cups, lotions, toothbrushes, and talcum powder?

A B C D

23. Consult Ms. Cheap's book in the bookstore and just jot down a few money-saving suggestions?

A B C D

There are indeed a lot of gray areas, but most things are pretty clear cut—if you are hurting someone else or going beyond the intent of a promotion, you are going too far. The bottom line is that honesty is the best policy, that having good ethics is a good thing, and that you can still be cheap within those confines. A lot of times just asking solves the problem. As one reader said: "Be very careful to practice what you preach so your children and grandchildren will learn the right thing to do."

Stay cheap! But ethical!